# John Abbot

*Birds, Butterflies and Other Wonders*

*John Abbot of Savannah.*

*Georgia.*

*America.*

ART *of*
NATURE

# John Abbot

## Birds, Butterflies and Other Wonders

PAMELA GILBERT

MERRELL HOLBERTON
PUBLISHERS LONDON
*and*
THE NATURAL HISTORY MUSEUM, LONDON

Unless otherwise stated, all photographs are taken from the books
and portrait collections of The Natural History Museum, London.
Thanks are due to Roxane Coombs and Harvard University for help
and permission to reproduce 'Notes on my Life'; Beverley D. Bishop
and Emory University, Atlanta, Georgia, for fig. 13; Gina Douglas and
the Linnean Society, London, for the Smith and Swainson letters and
some of Abbot's notes.

The Natural History Museum would like to thank the Hayward
Foundation for supporting the publication of this title in its
*Art of Nature* series.

First published in 1998 by
Merrell Holberton Publishers Ltd
Willcox House, 42 Southwark Street, London SE1 1UN
and
The Natural History Museum, London

British Library Cataloguing in Publication Data
Gilbert, Pamela, 1932–
    John Abbot : birds, butterflies and other wonders.
    – (Art of nature)
    1. Abbot, John – Criticism and interpretation    2. Natural
    history illustration    3. Painting, English    4. Painting, Modern
    – 17th–18th centuries – Great Britain
    I. Title    II. Abbot, John
    759.2

ISBN 1 85894 064 8

Designed by Roger Davies

Produced by Merrell Holberton Publishers
Printed and bound in Italy

Front jacket: *Orange tree butterfly*, detail (plate 22)
Back jacket: *Dragonfly* (plate 7)
Frontispiece: John Abbot, *Self-portrait*, *Insects of Georgia* (Francillon),
XVI, frontispiece

# Contents

# *Acknowledgements*

I have had much help in the production of this volume. It gives me considerable pleasure to thank publicly those who will allow me to do so.

First my thanks to Rex Banks, who encouraged me to start this book and, more importantly, to complete it! Particular thanks go to Paul Cooper, Ann Datta and Julie Harvey of The Natural History Museum libraries.

The scientific staff of the Departments of Botany, Entomology and Zoology (including the sub-department of Ornithology) were generous with their time, supplying me with current nomenclature to add, where possible, to Abbot's identifications.

Two people were particularly helpful in aiding me to trace Abbot paintings: Brenda Burgess, librarian of Knowsley Hall (Lord Derby's collection), and Monique Ducreux of the Bibliothèque Centrale du Muséum National d'Histoire Naturelle, Paris.

The excellent colour transparencies and the black-and-white photographs were produced by the staff of the photographic unit of The Natural History Museum; I thank them for their help and advice and their skill in handling some of the precious originals.

As always, the staff of the Department of Library and Information Services of The Natural History Museum were extremely helpful, often pointing out and obtaining references for me, and I thank them all. Special thanks must go to Gail Fordham, who put the original drafts on to disc and coped, without complaint, with my continuing revisions.

Pamela Gilbert .

The Natural History Museum would like to thank the Hayward Foundation for supporting the publication of this title in its *Art of Nature* series.

# *Introduction*

In July 1773, John Abbot (1751–1840), a young and talented Englishman, twenty-two years old, left England for America. He was to spend the rest of his life in Virginia and Georgia, collecting and painting natural history specimens for clients in England, continental Europe and America. For close on sixty-seven years he worked quietly and meticulously to supply collectors and other naturalists with specimens and with exquisite paintings and drawings of birds, insects and plants. Abbot's work was in constant demand throughout his long life, yet by the end of the nineteenth century he still remained virtually unknown in scientific circles. In spite of his prolific output, he had never sought recognition or fame for himself, and his name had appeared on only a single publication. The paintings of Abbot's contemporaries John James Audubon and Alexander Wilson are familiar to us all through their published works, yet Abbot was painting many of the birds described by Audubon long before Audubon began work, and it was Abbot who took Wilson collecting and supplied him with bird skins, data and illustrations.

Abbot himself left only the briefest of 'Notes on my Life', and some of the early biographical publications on his life have to be used with care. Three recent authors – Dr V. Rogers-Price, Dr M. Simpson and Dr R. Wilkinson – have done much to bring Abbot's work to a wider audience, but we still know tantalizingly little about his long and productive life.

The text of this book is intended not as a scholarly biography of John Abbot but rather as a summary of his activities as a collector and artist. It accompanies the reproductions of a selection of previously unpublished watercolours from The Natural History Museum's large collection of what John Lyon described as Abbot's "elegant and masterly drawings".

These exquisite paintings deserve a wider audience – not only because of their artistic merit but also for their importance to naturalists and to historians interested in Virginia and Georgia in the late eighteenth and early nineteenth centuries. Some of the species figured in these paintings had become extinct within forty years of Abbot's death. Abbot himself predicted changes in bird numbers as a result of the increase in human population and changes in farming practices, and some of the birds he painted are now extinct, or so rare as to be on the endangered list.

The author has had the pleasure of the company of this collection for many years, while employed in the libraries of The Natural History Museum, and hopes that this volume will serve to gain a wider appreciation of Abbot's undoubted talent.

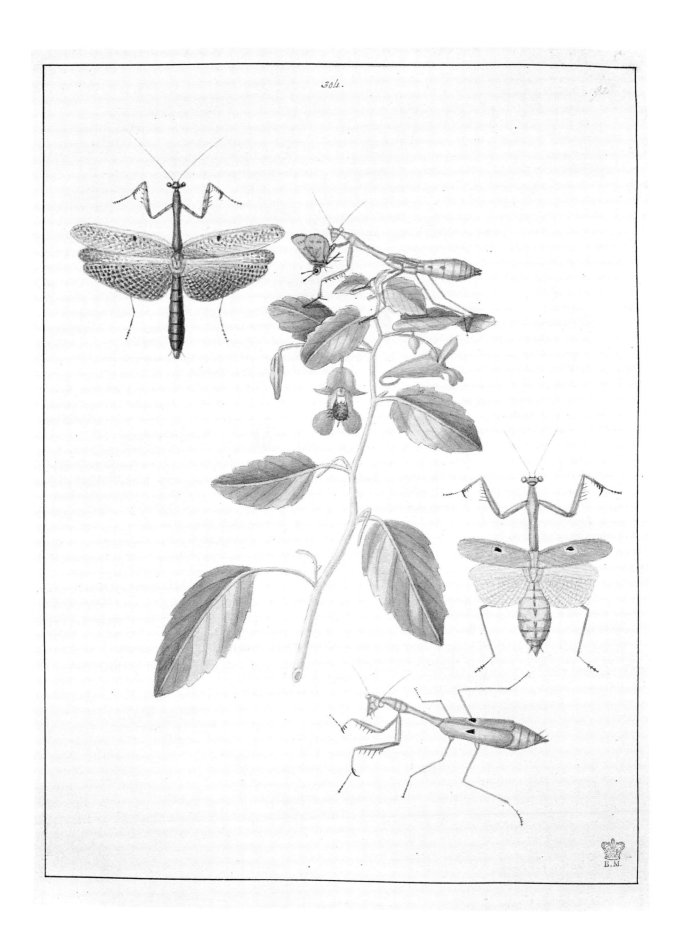

# John Abbot and his World

## "A Peculiar Liking for Insects"

PLATE 1 Green mantis *Mantis impatiens capensis*
Plant: Spotted Touch-me-not or Jewel weed

*It frequents different Plants and Flowers and Blossoms feeding on the insects it meets with, catching and holding them in its fore legs (like hands) to eat them. It shed its skin 31st August. The male flies about of an evening. This is not a common species.*

Plate size 23 × 30 cm. *Insects of Georgia* (Francillon), XV, p. [92], pl. 304

In his 'Notes on my Life'[1] Abbot tells us that he was born "in the year 1751, the first of June the old style[2] at the West End of the town, London in Bennet Street St James". Church records of St George's, Hanover Square, however, show his birth date as 31 May 1751. John Abbot's father, also John, was a lawyer who worked at the King's Bench Division court and had married an Ann Clousinger in 1749. John was the second son to be born; the first died before his birth. Two sisters, Elizabeth and Charlotte, followed, and another son, Thomas, completed the family.

The Abbots lived in the most fashionable part of London, in keeping with the status and income of a successful eighteenth-century lawyer. Bennet Street, St James, lying just behind Piccadilly, near the Ritz Hotel, is still fashionable, but the original houses have long disappeared. The family also spent time in another, rented, house in Turnham Green, about five miles west of central London – now part of Greater London, then in the country. The rent was £25 per year, but when the lease expired, when the young John was still a young boy, his father decided not to renew it. In the 'Notes', Abbot says that he had a drawing of the house, but there is no evidence that the drawing still exists.

We know nothing of John's formal education, nor indeed of his family life, but, given his father's position, he would probably have been educated at home by a private tutor in preparation for a profession – such as the law. John Abbot senior seems to have been a cultivated man and is described by his son as "having a valuable collection of prints, of some of the best Masters he also had many good paintings".

The young John shared his father's pleasures. He talks of his early love of books and an early taste for drawing – an interest that was presumably nurtured by ready access to his father's collections, and also by a Mr Bonneau. Jacob Bonneau (*fl.* 1741–86) was employed by Abbot to give his son "lessons of drawing at our own house". He seems to have been primarily an engraver, but some sources mention him using watercolours.[3] According to Abbot, "Mr Bonneau did not paint in watercolours, he only understood the rules of drawing and perspective", and adds, "he praised my drawings of insects."

John's interest in insects started when he was a child, and he was doubtless stimulated by what he saw during walks in the grounds and neighbourhood of Turnham Green. Abbot remembered, as a very young boy, long before he knew how to collect and keep insects, "knocking down a Libella and pining [sic] it". He was a born collector. On one of his walks he met a Mr Van Dest, "the famous flower painter",[4] who showed him a large collecting net, presumably a butterfly net, and gave him some rare insects. Abbot immediately went home and had a similar one made, thus improving his collecting technique.

In spite of the growing interest in natural history in the eighteenth century, the butterfly hunter was still looked upon as mildly dotty or regarded with contempt; the uninitiated might well look with suspicion upon a grown man leaping about and waving a net in the air.

The artist and entomologist Moses Harris (see p. 18) gives an account of a certain Lady (Elizabeth) Glanville (fl. 1654–1708), the earliest lady entomologist, who resided in the West Country and collected in the Bristol area:[5] "This fly [Glanville Fritillary] took its name from the ingenious Lady Glanville who memory had like to have suffered from her curiosity. Some relations that were disappointed by her will, attempted to set it aside by acts of lunacy, for they suggested that none but those who were deprived of their senses would go in pursuit of butterflies." Judge and jury were nevertheless satisfied with testimonies to the contrary, and established her will. Lady Glanville, it must be said, was something of an eccentric and her interest in butterflies probably added to the impression she gave: villagers suggested that she had been seen naked on the downs, and looking like a gypsy. However, Petiver (1701) recorded many specimens from her, and some of these specimens are still extant in the Petiver Collection in The Natural History Museum, London.

Another entomologist and artist, Joseph Dandridge (see p. 24), was also taken for a lunatic while collecting. He was said to know the best haunts of butterflies around London, and the story goes that a country labourer, watching him "leaping about", eventually caught him, to try to stop him runnning himself to death. The man's suspicions were confirmed when Dandridge was heard to gasp, "The Purple Emperor has gone, the Purple Emperor has gone!"[6]

Later, Edward Newman (1801–1879), in his *Grammar of Entomology* (1835), referring to the common opinion "that a person who could take an interest in pursuing a butterfly is a madman", wrote: "The collector of insects must, therefore, make up his mind to sink in the opinion of his friends; to be the object of the undisguised pity and ridicule of the mass of mankind."

However passionate a collector and accomplished a draughtsman, the young John was, in 1769, at the age of eighteen, articled to his father as a clerk for the five years necessary to qualify as an attorney. But he did not complete his articles: "Deeds Conveyances and Wills etc was but little to my liking when my thoughts were engrossed in Natural History", and it seems that his father must have accepted his wish to devote himself to natural history. Certainly, the 'Notes' make no mention of any parental opposition.

Bonneau was evidently a good teacher, and John Abbot learned his craft well. In 1770, aged nineteen, his talent was recognized when he exhibited two watercolour studies

PLATE 2 Mantis *Stagmomantis carolina* (Johannson)

*Female taken 6th September in Oak Woods and low Grounds of Savannah River. The Male flies in the evening. Its body is slender and wings longer than the Female here figured, it does not have wings till arrived at its full growth. I have taken several Females seemingly in full health and strength and pinned them in my Box, upon opening the box a few hours after have found several large maggots full fed that had eaten themselves out of the abdomen, and eat all the inside having been bred in the Mantis before it was taken and similar in caterpillars when Ichneumonid. Not common. Called in Savannah walking leaf.*

Plate size 11 × 14 cm. *Insects of Georgia* (Francillon), V, p. [10], pl. 4

4.

Mantis

TAB CXXXV

1 Entomological cabinet (likely to have been found in the homes of the nobility, such as the Duchess of Portland), from J.C. Schaeffer, *Elementa Entomologica* (1780), pl. 125

with illustrated publications of natural history.

The Duchess of Portland (Margaret Cavendish Bentinck), for example, spent about fifty years collecting everything and anything that took her fancy, and devoted large sums of money to buying specimens for her huge natural history cabinet (fig. 1); her home in Bulstrode, Buckinghamshire, was a haven for naturalists, and much of her social life was taken up with showing off her specimens to friends, and probably exchanging duplicates.

The French doctor, inventor of the thermometer, entomologist and author, R.-A.F. de Réaumur (1683–1757), wrote: "Some collectors were willing to pay such exorbitant prices for illustrations that they could have bought diamonds instead." (He also gave the advice: "Never trust what you hear – always look for yourself, it is also necessary to make drawings.")

Some owners collected merely for the sake of collecting or because it was fashionable among their friends, but others developed a true scientific interest in their acquisitions. No branch of science developed so rapidly as natural history during the 1700s, encompassing animals, minerals and plants. In England, botany had long been a particular subject of interest, partly because of the medicinal properties of plants. The first botanical garden in England had been founded in Oxford in 1621, and in 1673 the Society of Apothecaries established the Physic Garden in Chelsea.[8] European interest in gardening and the introduction of new plants from the Americas and further afield added to the botanical excitement.

Mr Rice, with whom Abbot was to have a fruitful friendship, gave him an *entrée* to the world of naturalists by introducing him to Dru Drury (1725–1804) (fig. 2), "who had been President of the Linnean Society & who then was allowed to have the best Collection of Insects both English and foreign of any one".[9] Drury, a goldsmith and jeweller by trade, had a workshop in the Strand and was to become the Queen's Goldsmith and Cutler

of lepidoptera at the London Society of Artists. Even more important for Abbot's later career, Bonneau "was acquainted with a Mr Rice a Teacher of Grammer, who had likewise been a Collector of Insects". Rice had a small cabinet of preserved specimens and, above all, knew many naturalists and collectors of insects.[7]

The eighteenth century brought a surge of interest in natural history. Throughout Europe, and perhaps especially in Britain, the collection of insects was taken up enthusiastically by the clergy, physicians, young ladies, and military officers during postings overseas. Scientific collections resulted, butterflies in particular exciting the interests of both the collector and artists. The aristocracy also acquired a passion for making collections of specimens and adorning their libraries

PLATE 3 Grasshopper, probably *Pardolophora phoenicoptera* Burmeister [*Gryllus obscura* Linn.]

*Taken 26th April in Pinewoods and old fields. Common – called in Savannah Red underwing Grasshopper.*

Size of drawing 11.5 × 15 cm. *Insects of Georgia*, V, p. [35], pl. 13

*13.*

Gr. obscurus Lin

*Lizars sc.*

DRURY.

2 Portrait of Dru Drury (1725–1804), from
W. Jardine (ed.), *Naturalist's Library*,
'Introduction to Mammalia', frontispiece

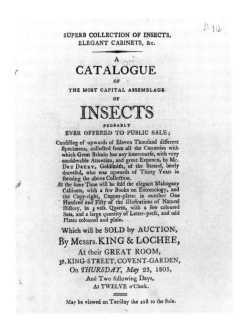

SUPERB COLLECTION OF INSECTS,
ELEGANT CABINETS, &c.

D. 11b

A
CATALOGUE
OF
THE MOST CAPITAL ASSEMBLAGE
OF
INSECTS
PROBABLY
EVER OFFERED TO PUBLIC SALE;

Confisting of upwards of Eleven Thousand different
Specimens, collected from all the Countries with
which Great Britain has any intercourse, with very
considerable Attention, and great Expence, by Mr.
DRU DRURY, Goldsmith, of the Strand, lately
deceased, who was upwards of Thirty Years in
forming the above Collection.

At the fame Time will be sold the elegant Mahogany
Cabinets, with a few Books on Entomology, and
the Copy-right, Copper-plates in number One
Hundred and Fifty of the Illustrations of Natural
History, in 3 vols. Quarto, with a few coloured
Sets, and a large quantity of Letter-prefs, and odd
Plates coloured and plain.

Which will be SOLD by AUCTION,
By Messrs. KING & LOCHEE,
At their GREAT ROOM,
38, KING-STREET, COVENT-GARDEN,
On *THURSDAY*, *May* 23, 1805,
And Two following Days,
At TWELVE o'Clock.

May be viewed on Tuesday the 21st to the Sale.

3 Dru Drury's sale catalogue, title page

to the King, but he was also at the centre of a wide circle of naturalists and lavished a fortune on what was reputedly the largest insect collection of the time. On his death, the sale catalogue, the first to be entirely devoted to insects, contained some 11,000 specimens (fig. 3). With the help of Drury and Rice, John Abbot no doubt met many of the leading collectors and naturalists of the time.

The meeting with Drury was a turning point in Abbot's life. Abbot was overwhelmed by Drury's collections and the cabinets in which they were housed, and later was allowed to borrow specimens to paint. He immediately had a cabinet made, which had twenty-six drawers, all with sliding glass tops; it cost six guineas, a princely sum. As a result of this meeting, Abbot increased his own collecting activities and began to purchase foreign insects, including a parcel of insects from Surinam in South America, no doubt through Drury. Abbot's father must have provided his son with a good allowance, for he was spending quite large sums of money to indulge his growing interest.

Drury not only took orders and requests for specimens newly arrived from abroad, but engaged intermediaries and employed collectors. Some of the largest cabinets, including Drury's own, were owned by those who had never collected a specimen of any kind themselves, but paid collectors to travel and collect for them. Europeans were becoming ever keener to know about the flora and fauna of the New World, as travellers returned with true accounts and sometimes bizarre descriptions of things they had seen. Commerce also began to expand, and with it wealth; merchants were accumulating fortunes from products arriving from the Americas. These new venturers, as well as the possessors of 'old money', became the patrons of those travelling to collect specimens of all kinds, including inevitably the hoped-for silver and gold. Some collectors sought their own sponsors, and left England with meagre sums in their pockets and explicit instructions on what to collect. The intention was, of course, that any additional material brought back could be sold to dealers in London or Liverpool on landing, but many never returned – succumbing to disease and climate. For this reason

PLATE 4  *Neuroptera: Chrysopidae* [*Phrygancea*]

*Taken 20th April in the woods, the antennae of the female is shorter than that of the male,*
*very common and called the Golden eye.*

Plate size 13 × 9 cm. *Insects of Georgia*, XII, p. [44], pl. +++666

4 Equipment given to ships' captains and other collectors by Dru Drury, from Drury's Letter Book

sponsors were not keen to give large sums of money to unknown entrepreneurs, and often gambled only on the more seasoned travellers. Drury and some of the European aristocracy preferred to deal with reliable collectors known to them – in Drury's case ships' captains. Drury sometimes dealt with what today would be regarded as a syndicate, where each member contributed a set amount and would expect desirable specimens for their cabinets.

Collectors were crossing the Atlantic in the hopes of making their fortune – or a better life – and to supply their patrons in Europe. Curiosity was considered an important part of a young man's baggage (the Continental Grand Tour stimulated the inquiring mind and the young aristocrat returned home with his luggage stuffed with statuary, paintings and natural history specimens). As a young man, Abbot was not immune from these influences and must have realised the potential of his own enthusiasms.

Ships' captains and crew members proved reliable collectors and were offered handsome sums of money

to collect specimens when in foreign ports. Drury made it his business to become acquainted with sea captains, keeping detailed records of their names and the names of their vessels, along with sailing times and destinations and the equipment that he had handed over to the crew (fig. 4). He supplied his collectors with boxes in which to transport the specimens, with printed instructions on what, where and how to collect different kinds of insects from around the ports.[10] He paid his collectors 6d. a specimen – quite an incentive to poorly paid crew – but made it clear that he would only pay for those in good condition. (Abbot was to charge the same price once his own collecting activities became established.) Drury was also in contact with insect-lovers and collectors – each trying to outdo the other. However, despite this rivalry, collectors frequently met to look at and exchange specimens and share news of departing and arriving ships.

Drury was a friend of the Duchess of Portland, and had obtained many specimens for her, and it seems likely that it was through his good offices that Abbot first met the Duchess and obtained access to her collection. She lent Abbot specimens to draw from her cabinet. As well as insects and other natural history specimens, it included valuables such as silver, porcelain and curios from around the world; it was reputed to be far more important than the collection in the British Museum. When, after her death in 1785, her collection was sold, the auction lasted thirty-eight days. Her museum had been curated by Daniel Carlsson Solander (1736–1782), naturalist and favourite student of Carl Linnaeus. Many of her specimens were purchased by Dru Drury and John Francillon,[11] another London jeweller, who had similarly developed an interest in insects and brought together a most prestigious collection from many parts of the world, and who in time was to become Abbot's agent in London (see p. 52).

Between 1770 and 1782, Drury published a magnificent three-volume work entitled *Illustrations of Natural History*,

PLATE 5 Dragonfly [*Libellula*]

*Taken 24th May, frequents swamps and parts adjacent. Not very common.*

Plate size 10 × 14 cm. *Insects of Georgia*, XII, p. [15], pl. 14

14.

Zur *g* akken Sep ef 11

17

5 Portrait of Moses Harris (1730–1788) – a self-portrait?

the plates for which were drawn by one of the leading entomological artists, Moses Harris.

Although Abbot's 'Notes' record that he bought Albin's work on *British Insects* (see p. 24), he does not mention Drury's book or, indeed, any of the fine colour plates being published in continental Europe at the time.[12] However, Drury's own records show that Abbot paid Drury £4. 18s. for a "best copy" of *Illustrations*, and had it bound himself before leaving for America.[13] Drury was always concerned to cover the cost of publishing his books. He writes to Captain Davies in 1770: "my work is coloured in general, in a common manner, the price of w[hi]ch is £2.12.6 agreeable to my advertisements, but there are some copies that I dispose of among my friends that are done in a superior manner ye price of w[hi]ch is £5.5.0 I dare not mention this in my advertisements, for if I did, I should never dispose of the common sort."[14]

In spite of a thriving transatlantic book trade,[15] Drury,

who published his own work, kept all his stock until many years after he completed the work, when he eventually passed it on to a bookseller. It seems likely that Abbot's parents would have sent the two later volumes of *Illustrations* out to him as soon as they were published, to enable him to complete the set.

Moses Harris (1730–1788) (fig. 5) was a painter and a highly respected engraver who was much in demand. His own entomological work, *The Aurelian*, was published in 1776 and ran to several editions. 'Aurelia' was the old name for butterfly (shining as gold) and was used as early as the 1600s to mean the chrysalis of the butterfly. The first entomological society to be established in London was called the Aurelian Society, and flourished in the 1740s. In his introduction to *The Aurelian*, Moses Harris gives a most colourful description of its demise in 1747:

"... the first hint I received was from Mr Moses Harris an uncle of mine, who was a member of the old Society of Aurelians which was held at The Swan Tavern, in Change Alley: I was then too young to be admitted as a member ... I was then but twelve years old – so obliged me to defer it, till Age should repair me with sufficient sagacity whereby I might become fitting for the company of that ingenious and curious body of people.

I was however deprived of that pleasure for not long after, the Great Fire happened in Cornhill, in which The Swan Tavern was burnt down together with the Societies valuable collections of insects, books, etc. and all the regalia; the Society was then sitting yet so sudden was the impetuous course of the Fire, that the flames beat against the windows, before they could get out of the room, many of them leaving their hats and canes."[16]

The second Aurelian Society was inaugurated in 1762 and counted among its members Harris and Drury. Moses Harris was secretary to the society and his book is "Dedicated to the president and the rest of the Gentlemen, the worthy members of the Aurelian Society".

Another significant entomologist, or 'Aurelian', of the period, who receives no mention from Abbot, is Benjamin Wilkes (died 1749). Wilkes died before Abbot was born, but his works would surely have been seen by

*5.*

PLATE 6  Dragonfly [*Libellula*]

*Taken 20th April, frequents swamps and rice fields etc. Rare.*

Plate size 10 × 14 cm. *Insects of Georgia*, XII, p. [6], pl. 5

6 Portrait of Carl Linnaeus (1707–1778)

hardly have avoided discussion on the work of the great Swedish naturalist Carl Linnaeus (1707–1778) (fig. 6). In his *Systema Naturae*, first published in 1735, Linnaeus had introduced the classification of all plants and animals according to a binomial system. This work was followed by others, but it took some time before Linnaeus's system was accepted; the tenth edition of the book, published in 1758, is now universally accepted as the starting-point for modern zoological nomenclature.

Oemler, Abbot's friend in Savannah (see p. 54), took the view that Abbot knew nothing of Linnaeus, but it is difficult to believe that he was entirely ignorant of Linnaeus's work. Drury, for example, was an enthusiastic supporter of the Linnean systematics, and although his *Illustrations of Natural History* did not give scientific names to the plates or in the text, the index follows the Linnaean system. Indeed, a letter to Linnaeus in August 1770 leaves us in no doubt of his admiration:

"Most excellent Sir
I cannot better express the strong inclination I have of testifying my respect to you as ye greatest Master of Natural history now existing than by presenting you a copy of a work I have just published here. Believe me Sir it is not from vanity I take the liberty of making you this offering, nor, poor as it is (for I am truly sensible of its defects), would I take it to any person that is inferior to Linnaeus in the study of nature. But to whom should I pay my acknowledgements of this sort but to the Father of Natural History?

You Sir; I consider as that Father, and therefore I beseech your kind acceptance here of, a circumstance that will do me great honor and favor and at the sametime countenance my weak endeavours to promote a study that I must confess to prefer to any other.... Permit me also to take this opportunity to congratulate you on the effects which your Systema had had among the followers of Natural history here in London."[18]

Abbot at Drury's home or at the home of the Duchess of Portland. Wilkes gave the exact date of when and where he had collected a specimen, and the date of metamorphosis of the species he bred. Abbot had bred insects from an early age, and the notes associated with his paintings were always very detailed. Information of the kind given by Wilkes would certainly have influenced the way he worked.

With Drury, Abbot would surely have joined friends at the coffeehouses where, in the absence of the formal natural history society, groups of naturalists and collectors would meet to discuss common interests and exchange or take delivery of specimens they had ordered. Coffeehouses were first established in London in 1652 and quickly became fashionable meeting places.[17] They provided centres for gossip as well as for more erudite exchange of ideas, and played an important part in the social life of the time. At such meetings, Abbot could

PLATE 7 Dragonfly *Anex* sp. [*Libellula*]

*Taken 23rd March frequents Fields and adjoining low grounds, or swamps. Common on some parts, but not in general.*

Plate size 12.4 × 14 cm. *Insects of Georgia*, XII, p. [7], pl. 6

## 6

Wilkinson (1984) discusses Abbot's apparent ignorance of the Linnean method in some detail, and shows evidence of Abbot's use of J. Berkenhout's *Natural History of Great Britain and Ireland* (1769) which follows Linnaeus's methods. Some of Abbot's spellings are the same as those of Berkenhout, and he follows Berkhout's descriptions very closely.

George Edwards's bird books, which Abbot's father purchased for him, also had an index of Linnaean names, and the Danish systematist Johann Christian Fabricius (1745–1808), a student of Linnaeus, selected a number of Abbot's American specimens from Francillon's collection and included them in his most famous book, *Entomologia emendata et aucta*, published in 1793. Often described as one of the best entomologists of the eighteenth century, Fabricius's enthusiasm for entomology probably derived from Linnaeus, and he was eventually to describe more of the common insects of Europe than anyone else except his mentor.[19] Francillon wrote to one of his correspondents in Manchester, in 1787: "I have had the pleasure of seeing Mr. Fabricius in London, he was with me one day last week, ten o'clock in the morning until nine at night and described many of the lepidoptera."[20] It seems more than likely that he passed the same information on to Abbot.

Among Drury's friends and acquaintances who were to influence and help the young Abbot was Henry Smeathman (*fl.* 1750–87), a young man of Abbot's own age. Smeathman, a professional plant and insect hunter who travelled abroad to fulfill commissions, had heard of Abbot through Mr Rice, and introduced himself, probably at Drury's home, as a "brother flycatcher". By his own admission, Abbot was a shy young man, "not fond of strangers", but he quickly took to young Smeathman. Drury was instrumental in sending Smeathman to West Africa with various commissions for insects, both on his own behalf and on that of other collectors. Smeathman's expenses were defrayed by a group of subscribers which included the Duchess of Portland who put up £100. The money invested by these sponsors would cover both travelling expenses and the insects he was to collect.

In the 'Notes', Abbot writes: "This Mr Smeathman went to Africa on an intention chiefly to collect insects, he stayed 2 or 3 years, & returned to England after I left it, he made a publication on it,[21] particular on account of the Ants, and the large hillocks they make there, he was going out there again, as Deputy Governor, to a British Establishment there, but was taken with a fever and died."

There were indeed hazards for these early naturalists and explorers. The botanist and entomologist John Banister (1650–1692) went to Virginia as a young clergyman but slipped, fell and was killed while collecting plants. He was the first to observe scientifically the insects of North America,[22] and, as a result of receiving five insects from Banister, the English naturalist and collector J. Petiver (1658–1718), gave a paper on the subject to the Royal Society.[23]

Abbot, fired with enthusiasm by his meetings with Smeathman and others, was beginning to see where his destiny lay – not with the law but with insects and with painting. It was becoming apparent that he could make money from these pursuits, or at least earn enough to keep body and soul together, and he began to trade in a modest way, selling all his duplicate English insect specimens "at a good price". Smeathman had a small collection, which included a Purple emperor butterfly, even then quite a rarity. Abbot had never seen one before and paid Smeathman a guinea for it, an almost staggering sum by today's standards. However, while out walking he collected a hornet moth for which a gentleman offered him two guineas. "I thought the offer so liberal I let him have it." These were large sums of money for a young man to be dealing in.

Abbot may have begun to make money, but his father

Plate 8  Crab  *Ocypode quadrata* (Fabricius 1787) [*Cancer*]
*Sand crab, it frequents the sand on the Islands and Salts near Savannah.*

Plate size 20.5 × 27 cm. *Insects of Georgia*, XV, p. [21], pl. 1

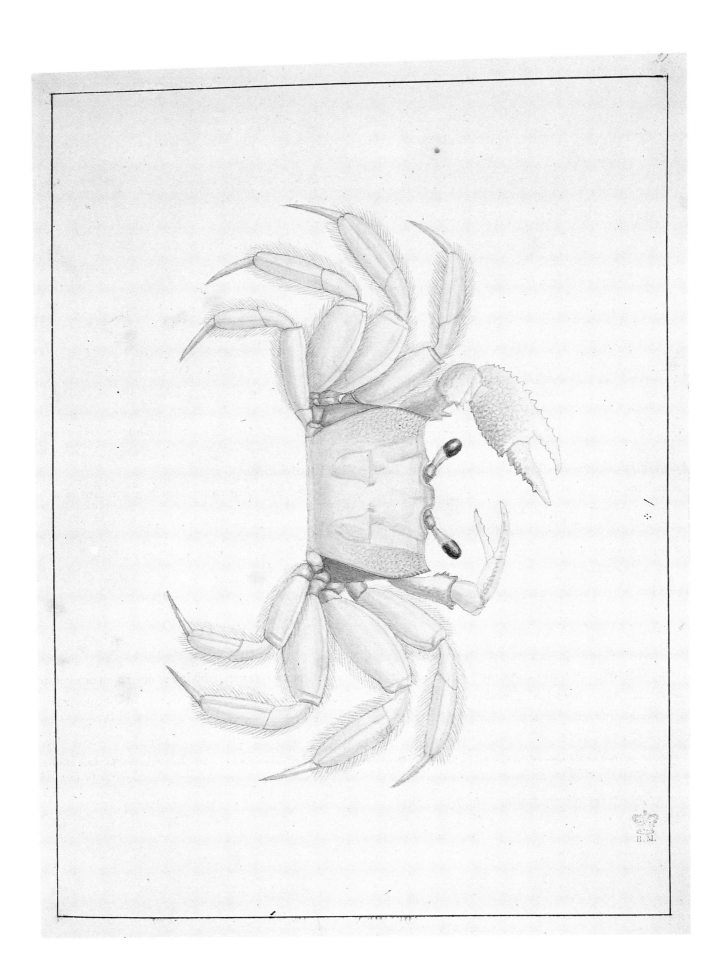

7 Portrait of Eleazar Albin (*fl.* 1713–59)

must undoubtedly have helped him. He was now able to buy books. The publishing world had begun to take advantage of the growing interest in natural history and had started to include coloured plates in their publications. Some were magnificent; others were poor. (In 1766, when *The Young Lady's Introduction to Natural History* was published, a review article noted that "even grown gentlemen may profit by the persuit of it".) Peter Collinson (1691–1768), a Quaker cloth merchant and naturalist who imported seeds and plants through his trade connections in North America, and later through John Bartram, the great American botanist and seedsman, wrote in 1747: "We [the English] are very fond of all natural history; they sell the best of any books in England."

Abbot started with Eleazar Albin's (fig. 7) splendid *A Natural History of English Insects* (1720), the first book on insects to be published in England with hand-coloured engravings.

In his preface Albin describes himself as a teacher of drawing and painting in watercolours, and says that the more he used plants and insects as subjects for his paintings, the more his interest in them grew. Weiss (1926) states that Albin had been employed by Joseph Dandridge (1660–1745),[24] a collector of insects, to paint caterpillars. However, a Dandridge manuscript in the British Library carries the label "A book of about 63 caterpillars drawn by Joseph Dandridge",[25] and since Dandridge was an accomplished artist (a silk-screen printer and designer of patterns for silk and damask),[26] it would seem unlikely that he would employ another artist to work for him, particularly one that did not share the same entomological knowledge. Albin was undoubtedly influenced by Dandridge, and Bristowe (1967) mentions that Albin copied many of Dandridge's spider drawings – without attribution.

Dandridge was one of the earliest entomologists, and a passionate collector whose fine collection was eventually incorporated into that of the physician, collector and naturalist Sir Hans Sloane (1660–1753), whose own collection of natural history from Jamaica, together with acquired collections, was to form part of the nucleus upon which the British Museum was founded in 1753 – collections with which the young Abbot would surely have been familiar. There are specimens from Dandridge's collection in The Natural History Museum, London.[27]

Abbot describes his early book-buying:

"I had bought Albins history of the changes of Insects coloured which was of great use to me, he had also published 3 vols of Birds – my father went to purchase it, at an Auction[28] of Books, but did not & instead bought 4 vols of Mr Edwards Birds, but so much superior to Albins, I was much pleased with the change, but there was 3 more to be published later [*Gleanings of Natural History* (1758–64)], we went together to his house to buy them. I carried some of my Drawings with me, he praised

PLATE 9 Crab [*Cancer*]

*Taken off the coast of Savannah.*

Plate size 20.6 × 27 cm. *Insects of Georgia*, XV, p. [23]

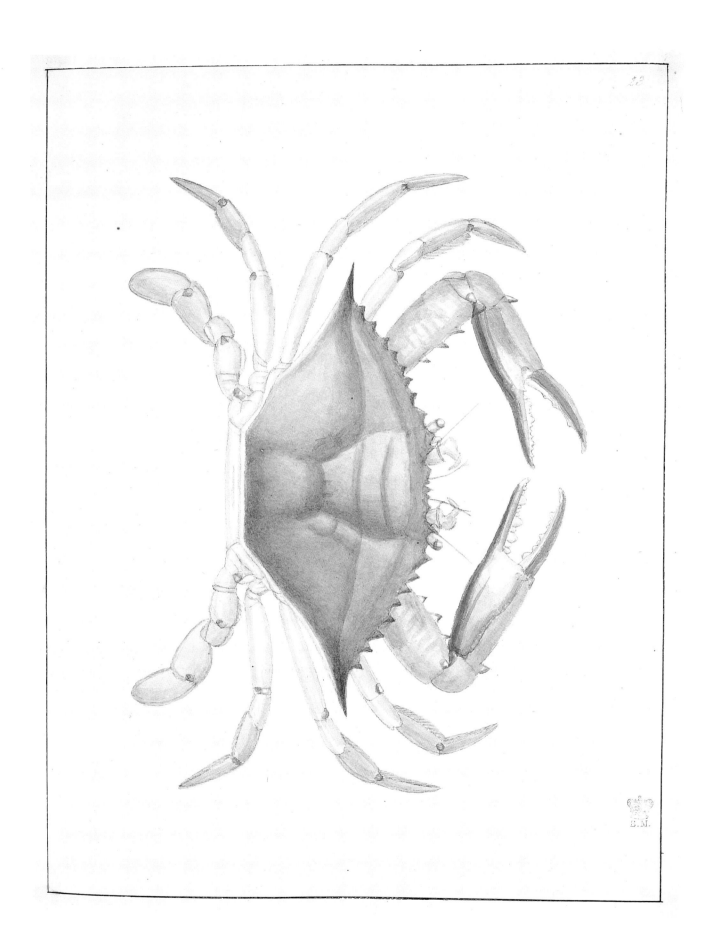

8 Portrait of George Edwards (1694–1773)

9 Plates from George Edwards's *A Natural History of
Uncommon Birds* (1743–51)

them much and desired me by all means to continue drawing, saying no doubt I would be a publisher hereafter of
some work on Natural history."

George Edwards's (fig. 8) *A Natural History of Uncommon Birds* (1743–51) was one of the most important bird
books of the time, and also (some of the plates were
enhanced with butterflies (fig. 9)) of entomology.[29]
Edwards had been a tradesman in early life, but preferred
the study of science and had travelled extensively. When
he returned to England in 1733, he settled in London and
successfully sought the patronage of Sir Hans Sloane.
Sloane supported Edwards's application for the post of
librarian to the Royal College of Physicians, and shortly
after his appointment Edwards began work on the paintings that were to be used to illustrate his major work on
birds. These illustrations earned him the Gold Medal of
the Royal Society, to which he was later elected a Fellow.

Plate 10  Belted kingfisher  *Ceryle alcyon* [*Aleedo Meyon*]

A similar painting went to the Chethams Library and to Francillon.

Plate size 20 × 40 cm. *Birds of Georgia* (Rothschild bequest), pl. 93

*Belted Kingsfisher*

With Edwards's praise, Abbot could not be asking for better encouragement.

Edwards's introduction to the book would have interested Abbot:

"It is not unreasonable to expect that a work of this nature should be highly laboured and finished in the colouring part, because it would greatly raise the price of it, as colouring work in London, when highly finished, comes very dear ..."

adding:

"Natural History cannot in any degree be perfect without figures; therefore I think we should promote drawing, in all such young people as seem to have a liking for it. No need think it an amusement beneath his dignity."

Edwards knew what he was talking about, for he had drawn, engraved and coloured nearly all his own plates. As a result, he was able to give the most detailed instructions to colourists for hand-colouring his engravings. Edwards's style was conventional for his time, showing his birds perched rather woodenly on tree stumps with little additional foliage, but Abbot considered his bird illustrations superior to Albin's and was later to be influenced by them in his own paintings of birds.

Perhaps even more important for Abbot's immediate future was a gift of Mark Catesby's *The Natural History of Carolina, Florida and the Bahama Islands* (1731–43): "About this time Lady Honeywood, widow of General Honeywood made me a present of Catesby's Nat. Hist. of Carolina a subscription Copy £20 price,[30] all this you may suppose increased my love in general for Nat. history."

Here was another magnificent volume to fuel the young man's enthusiasm, and may well have contributed to his desire to go to America. Mark Catesby (1683–1749) was illustrating local North American fauna some sixty years before Abbot. Abbot, on the other side of the Savannah River, was to record some 160 species of birds to Catesby's 90 – although Catesby strongly maintained that few birds had escaped him!

Books such as these, both 'plain and coloured', were published by subscription, necessitating hard work on the part of the author to secure a list of subscribers. This list would be printed in the published work, and the commitment of prestigious names was an encouragement to others to appear among them. Albin, for example, listed among his subscribers the Duke and Duchess of Beaufort, the Earl of Derby, Charles Dubois Esq., FRS, Treasurer to the Honorable East India Company, and Mr John Marshall, Maker of Optik glasses to his Majesty at the Archimedes in Ludgate Street. In addition, Albin dedicated each plate to a subscriber. The book went into several editions, and although some of the first subscribers withdrew their support, the names of new subscribers were added to the later editions, and new dedications appeared on the plates.

Another influence on the young Abbot's interest in natural history and on his determination to travel may well have been that of the naturalist and traveller Joseph Banks (1743–1820). Banks, only eight years older than Abbot, had already visited Newfoundland in 1766. He left to go round the world with Captain James Cook in 1768, and arrived home in 1771, a full two years before Abbot left for America. By the time they left, when Abbot was seventeen, the expedition would certainly have been the subject of intense interest to London's naturalists, especially as Banks had insisted on an artist accompanying the crew to record the natural history specimens that they collected. Banks's collections, herbarium and library were always open to visiting scientists,

PLATE 11  Passenger pigeon  *Ectopistes migratorius* (Linn.) [*Columba Migratoria*]

Now extinct. A similar plate with a slightly different stance was in the Chethams Library collection, now in a private collection in USA.

Plate size 20 × 40 cm. *Birds of Georgia* (Rothschild bequest), pl. 43

*Passenger Pigeon.*

and his London home at 32 Soho Square became a meeting-place for naturalists and others. By the time the expedition returned, Abbot's collecting activities and watercolours had made him known to London's circle of naturalists; their cabinets were open to him, he had been given several commissions to paint specimens, and had began to accumulate a sizeable portfolio of his own.[31] He would have been drawn to the huge collection of unfinished Australian drawings of Banks's expedition artist, Sydney Parkinson (1745–1771), who had died at sea during the return voyage, which were being worked on in Soho Square.

By the time he was twenty-two, Abbot had decided to give up the security of the law for good, and go to America: "In the beginning of the year 1773, I was determined to come to America, but what part to choose was the only matter to determine on. A Frenchman & his son come from Orleans, they praised that very much, but I had met with a hist of Virginia painted in such glowing Colours, & the Voyage there being much shorter I determined on Virginia."

The "history of Virginia" was probably Robert Beverley's *History and Present State of Virginia*, published in 1705. Some of Drury's letters mention Abbot's intention to go to Virginia; he wrote to Smeathman, in Africa, that Abbot was to depart to collect insects for a dealer in King Street, mentioning a Mr Martyn: "Young Abbot is going to Virginia on the same purpose with yourself – he is to collect for the dealer in King Street."[32]

Thomas Martyn (*fl.* 1760–1816) was an author, dealer, and illustrator of a number of books on shells and butterflies. His *Psyche*, published in 1797, contains his own paintings of insects from Georgia, which were collected there for him by Abbot. At his premises in King Street he bought and sold natural history specimens. He was one of Abbot's sponsors, but there is no record of the number of specimens to reach him.

Abbot started to make preparations for his voyage. He was embarking on a new and decidedly precarious way of earning a living. The journey by sea would itself be hazardous, as the fate of some of his collections was to show, and, although others had gone before him, both to America and to other countries of the world, to record all that they saw by collecting and painting specimens, his predecessors had usually been employed to do a job of work and had then returned home. John Abbot left to settle in Virginia with some commissions for specimens, but for him there was no certain future.

Abbot's father was relatively rich, and he himself seems to have had money to spend, so we must assume that he sailed from England with a well-lined purse; he may well have had the promise of an allowance, if only until he was settled in his new career. The indications are that his father was supportive of this venture before he left England; it seems likely that he sent books out to his son in America, and we do know that they kept in touch by letter.

Even the first settlers in America in the sixteenth century had collected and painted natural history specimens. In 1585, Walter Raleigh's flotilla of ships arrived at Roanoke Island, now in North Carolina. The expedition, instigated by Elizabeth I and under the command of Sir Richard Grenville, was the first Anglo-Saxon attempt at settlement in the New World.[33] Grenville had taken a degree in mathematics at Oxford in 1579, and the company included another mathematician, and scientist, Thomas Harriot (1560–1621), who had been appointed surveyor to the expedition, as well as John White, an artist. Here were the beginnings of a new tradition: the artist specially appointed to make pictorial records from newly discovered territories. White was "sent at no small expense, Mr whith [sic] a skilful and ingenious painter to take the situation of the Country, and to paint, from the Life, the Figures and habits of the natives and their way of living."[34]

White's 112 drawings included birds, fish, insects and plants of the colony then known as Virginia.[35] Both Grenville and Harriot were also interested in botany,

Plate 12  Summer tanager  *Piranga rubra* [*Tanagra Astiva*]

Plate size 20 × 40 cm. *Birds of Georgia* (Rothschild bequest), pl. 52

Summer Tanager.

10 American Swallowtail butterfly, drawing by John White, from Hulton and Quinn (1964)

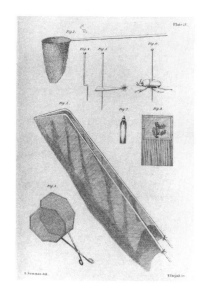

zoology and anthropology. Thomas Harriot and John White were to publish *The plant and animal life of all beasts, birds, fowls, fruits and roots and how they may be useful*, and Harriot *A Briefe and true Report on the New found land of Virginia* (1590) (fig. 10).

Earlier arrivals in other parts of America had also recorded its natural history. The Spaniard Fernandez de Oviedo y Valdes (1478–1557) had written a treatise which included many American birds, mammals and insects, and the Frenchman Jean de Levt (1534–1611) described plants and animals from Central and South America. Interest in the curiosities of the country began to grow.

Abbot would need collecting equipment: "I sold my Cabinet of Insects, drawings etc. I had 3 smaller Wainscot Cabinets made to bring with me."

The paraphernalia required for collecting was considerable; as well as the three cabinets, boxes of equipment would have included pins, breeding cages, nets, cork, cork-lined boxes (figs. 11 and 12) and suitable clothing. If, as Drury indicates, Abbot was also intending to collect birds, he would have taken dissecting tools and possibly a gun. Gunsmiths in London had a good

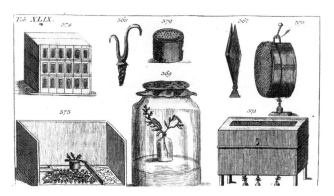

11 Collecting paraphernalia, from E. Newman, *Grammar of Entomology* (1813)

12 Breeding cages, from J.C. Schaeffer, *Elementa entomologica* (1780)

reputation; at the very least he may well have taken advice on the type of gun and shot he would need.

The frontispiece of Moses Harris's *Aurelian* (1766) provides a vivid portrait of an early eighteenth-century collector of insects. The nets are in evidence and the collector (supposed to be Harris himself) has his pincushion to hand and a cork-lined box in which to pin

PLATE 13 White (Ivory) billed woodpecker
*Campephilus principalis* (Linn.) [*Picus Principalis*]

Nearing extinction – last confirmed sighting 1950? Quite common in Abbot's time. One of three known Abbot plates of this species, each with a slightly different stance. His copy to Chethams Library is now in private hands; another copy was sent to Francillon.

Plate size 20 × 40 cm. *Birds of Georgia* (Rothschild bequest), pl. 37

White billed Woodpecker.

13 Self-portrait (?) of John Abbot (?),
charcoal, Emory University, Atlanta

14 Use of the umbrella for collecting, from C.V. Riley, *Directions for Collecting and Preserving Insects* (1892)

his specimens. A century or so later, a chapter on collecting in Newman's *Grammar of Entomology* (1835) deals extensively with the use of different kinds of nets, pins and desirable clothing. The common clap-net and forceps are clearly described and illustrated. Clothing styles had changed since Abbot set out for the New World in the 1770s, though much of the equipment would have been the same. The fashionable top hat was sometimes worn by the collector in the field – allegedly lined with cork and used to transport the pinned specimens home. Perhaps Abbot is doing just this in one of the (supposed) self-portraits (fig. 13). There is no firm evidence that this charcoal sketch of an entomologist carrying his tray around his neck, on which to pin specimens, is by Abbot, but it was among a collection of Abbot illustrations

bought by Emory University, Georgia. The illustration of an umbrella used as a catching tray for insects beaten from trees and shrubs is well known (fig. 14), but is from a slightly later period than Abbot. Umbrellas were widely used in this way; though the one shown in the Schaeffer plate of 1789 (fig. 15) looks more like a lady's parasol.

Drury normally supplied his collectors with the necessary paraphernalia for both collecting and transporting specimens. He did not want damaged specimens and was meticulous in his instructions to the collectors. One can assume, therefore, that John Abbot sailed for America with similar equipment, and it is a reasonable guess that some of it was supplied by Drury. He certainly also took supplies of paints and pigments and good quality paper with him. John Francillon (see p. 52), sent

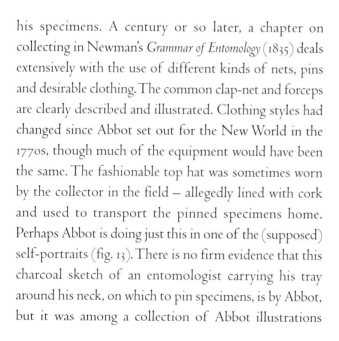

PLATE 14 Hooping (Whooping) Crane *Grus americana* (Linn.) [*Ardea Americana*]
Now an endangered species, a breeding population of some 100 birds.

Plate size 20 × 40 cm. *Birds of Georgia* (Rothschild bequest), pl. 106

Hooping Crane.

INSTRVMENTA.                    TAB.CXXXIII

15 Examples of equipment that might have been taken by John Abbot to America, from J.C. Schaeffer, *Elementa Entomologica* (1780), pl. 133

him pins and paints at fairly frequent intervals but after Francillon's death in 1816 he had to find other sources. In 1835 he wrote to a friend and fellow naturalist, William Swainson: "If you approve of the long slim pins in preference to these common ones please to send me some as I cannot procure them in Savannah I have formaly received from Mr Francillon a more middle size (slimmer) pin in length, which I prefer to either for small insects."[36]

Commissions were essential if Abbot was to earn his living across the Atlantic, and several naturalists, including Drury and Thomas Martyn, gave him orders for specimens. The Royal Society gave him an introductory letter requesting observations and specimens of natural history from Virginia. In the eighteenth and nineteenth centuries the Royal Society would often arrange for travellers of repute to carry letters of introduction from the Secretary of State for the Colonies (at that time the Earl of Dartmouth) to resident Governors abroad.[37] The Society dominated scientific interests of the time. Established in 1660, and incorporated by Royal Charter in 1662, to promote research in the sciences, it was not the élitist society it is today, but its influence was strong, and it guided the scientific community in America until home-grown American philosophical and natural history societies were born. Fellows of the Royal Society in London were in touch with work being done in the colonies. Some of these New World scholars had left the colleges of Oxford and Cambridge and were establishing new seats of learning. The Royal Society honoured some of these scholars by election to the Society. (John Winthrop Jnr, eldest son of the first governor of Massachusetts, was the first of these to be elected, in 1663.) Abbot would not have had sufficient standing as a naturalist to have been elected to a fellowship of the Royal Society before he left.

Drury also gave Abbot introductions to two of his correspondents in Virginia and, about two months before Abbot left, wrote to the Reverend Devereux Jarrat, requesting him to aid Abbot in collecting ("the principal articles he intends to collect are birds, plants, insects, fishes animals etc minerals etc") and on the same day to Dr James Greenway, saying: "he may be able to improve your knowledge of insects."[38]

By April 1773, Abbot was ready. He arranged his passage on the *Royal Exchange*, captained by a Mr Woodford, and paid 25 guineas for his passage. The ship had been overhauled and repaired but there were delays and she was not finally ready to sail until July. Abbot's luggage was taken on board and he was ready to go.

During the period of delay, he had not been idle. He had been recommended to a Mr Humphrey (1739–1826),

PLATE 15  Blue jay  *Cyanocitta cristata* [*Corvus Cristatus*]

Common in the United States of America.

Plate size 20 × 40 cm. *Birds of Georgia* (Rothschild bequest), pl. 23

Blue Jay.

archaeologist and collector of insects, to draw shells, and was glad of the chance to earn some money; he painted the figures on vellum, and charged one guinea for each drawing. Abbot obviously knew his worth; Humphrey was delighted with the results and tried to persuade him to delay his journey and continue with the illustrations, but time had run out: "One Morning I went to the Coffee house to know when the Ship would sale, was told she had sailed, but might perhaps overtake her in the River [the Thames] before she got out to Sea."

With his belongings already on board and his future slipping away, Abbot described himself as "a good deal surprised and alarmed". However, he hired a post-chaise and, collecting his father, mother and seven-year-old Tommy, set off to try and overtake the ship. They spied her at one point but she was too far ahead for them to catch up. Their only hope was to reach Deal on the east coast of Kent, the *Royal Exchange*'s last port of call before the ship finally sailed for America. They reached Deal in a great state of agitation and apprehension, to find the ship lying offshore. Abbot lost no time in hiring a boat to take him out to the *Royal Exchange*, leaving his mother in tears and master Tommy still in a high state of excitement over the journey. In the event, the ship did not sail for another three days. The captain and some of the passengers returned to shore for a time, but Abbot was taking no chances and stayed firmly on the ship, preparing himself for the journey ahead. He would never see his parents and family again.

Abbot found himself one of eight cabin passengers when the *Royal Exchange* eventually sailed. Among them was a Mr Parke Goodall and his new English wife, Mary. Goodall was returning to restock his country store and ordinary,[39] located some 100 miles from the James River, which he owned with his brother. He had a large cargo of merchandise which had been provided by a wealthy uncle in London.

On 9 September 1773, the *Royal Exchange* arrived at the James River. After six weeks at sea, and a brief stop in Madeira where he failed to "meet with any Butterfly or Moth", Abbot set foot on the land he had dreamed of. He must have been filled with excitement and apprehension. Most of his life had been spent in fashionable London, with all the comforts of an excellent home where his only, minor privations would have been those encountered during collecting excursions into the country-side. In spite of the fact that Virginia was a thriving colony, and already had the longest history of English settlement in what was soon to become the United States of America, there could have been little comparison with home. Under its charter from the original settlement of Jamestown in 1667, Virginia had been granted most of the unexplored lands west of the Atlantic seaboard to the Mississippi River and beyond. Virginians were to be leaders in the War of American Independence (1775–83) and in the events leading up to it. Abbot was soon to find the times becoming alarming.

Drury had given Abbot an introduction to a minister, the Revd Jarrat, in Dinwiddee County, assuring him that Jarrat would give him help in settling and finding a home of his own. However, his friends Parke Goodall and his wife had invited Abbot to stay with them, and Abbot decided to accept their invitation, rather than seek out a stranger. On arrival, Goodall made the acquaintance of a Mr Balfour who owned a small sloop and was about to sail up the James River to the by then deserted Jamestown to buy wheat for shipment to England. Balfour offered to take Goodall, his wife and Abbot as passengers. From Jamestown, they hired chairs and a carrier to take them all to Goodall's home in Hanover County, which was to become Abbot's headquarters for the next two years. The area was found to be sickly "with fevers and

PLATE 16 Bald eagle *Haleetus leucocephalus* (Linn.) [*Falco Leucocephalus*]

These are now seriously diminished in numbers, but in 1827 Abbot had commented that it had become rare. Another similar painting of this bird is in the Houghton Library, Harvard University.

Plate size 20 × 40 cm. *Birds of Georgia* (Rothschild bequest), pl. 2

*Bald Eagle.*

fluxes" but during his stay in Virginia Abbot "was very fortunate not to have been ill".

Virginia was something of a disappointment. Abbot found neither the numbers nor the variety of insects that he had hoped for, though within a short time of his arrival he managed to collect over 800 specimens and produced a report on the geology of the area for transmission to Drury. He knew nothing of American naturalists or collectors: men such as John Bartram (1699–1777), for example, the first American to become involved in botanical collecting. A Quaker from Philadelphia, Bartram sent seeds and plants to Peter Collinson in London for thirty-five years, and collected for Linnaeus. Linnaeus described him as the greatest of field botanists. In 1765 Bartram was appointed King's Botanist to George III, with a pension of £50 a year.[40]

On top of everything else, the first cabinet of insects that Abbot shipped to London was lost when the ship foundered and sank off the English coast. Despair overtook him and he decided to return to England. It was not only the lack of insects that worried him; "the times [were] now becoming very troublesome". Virginia was determined to sever links with England, there was considerable unrest, and revolution was in the air. Abbot took himself off to the courthouse where shipping transactions were conducted, but failed to arrange for his return and gave up the idea: "The Captain was not coming, I gave it out." It must have been a traumatic time for the young man.

A second cargo of insects was lost: "The Colinies having appointd a day after which all Intercourse with England, was to be stopped, I fixed up another Cabinet of Insects to send to England, they was on board the boat on the River to the ship, when a terrible September storm arose in the night, and the boat was lost together with my insects again."

Eventually, a third collection from Virginia made safe passage and was delivered to Drury. In spite of Abbot's worries about what he considered small numbers of insects, Drury seems to have been more than pleased with the specimens that had been shipped to him. Not only had Abbot sent him some 570 different species but the specimens had been carefully pinned and had arrived in excellent condition. Early on, Abbot had also begun to illustrate the specimens that he collected, and had started the practice, which was to stay with him all his life, of recording, with his illustrations, any relevant information, particularly regarding habitat and breeding. Drury had urged him to try and breed from the larvae of his insects, and wrote:

"I confess I think you have been industrious to collect 570 species in so short a time … . The truth is nobody here knows what the country produces because nobody has ever tried to obtain insects by that method. Let me ask you if your speculations are intended to be confined to insects? Will you not search into other parts of Natural History? particularly in Mineralia. I am strongly of the opinion that this part of nature will attend as much business as any other … the stones of America also we are as ignorant of as the insects. If you search diligently into that class perhaps you may make discoveries of great importance to mankind."[41]

Drury asked Abbot to search for gold and pearls, and in 1774 wrote in reply to Abbot's report on the lack of minerals: "of your account of the Mineralia Im quite satisfied with I believe there are very few to be found in your part of the world."[42]

Drury, like other collectors and investors, was obsessed with the discovery of gold or other precious metals; he was convinced that gold could easily be found in the rivers,

PLATE 17 (Little) Blue heron *Egretta caerulea* [*Ardea Carulea*]
A similar plate is in the Smithsonian Archives, but the basal vegetation is different and here there are no distant house and trees as there are in the Smithsonian copy.

Plate size 20 × 40 cm. *Birds of Georgia* (Rothschild bequest), pl. 110

*Blue Heron.*

and his instructions for collectors included notes on precious metals. He urged Smeathman, collecting for him in Sierra Leone, to search for gold: "Minerals or mines may be found – where does all the gold come from that is brought to Europe? I am sure there must be some source or store of it whence it is washed down rivers and is this store never to be discovered? ... how much I should rejoice if it was at ye last hour of my life to be discovered." And, needing gemstones for his jewellery business, he wrote again: "I have lately heard that emeralds are frequently found there [West Africa], if you therefore find any green stones pray send them to me ... and for stones that are quite black and hard, preserve them with great care ... they must be black ... and without any milky spots on them, but of a regular even colour." Smeathman found neither emeralds nor diamonds – nor gold! Many others also searched, no doubt hoping for instant financial reward, but there was more disappointment than reward.

John William Lewin, whom Drury had dispatched to Australia to collect for him, wrote to Drury in 1803: "I hope you will never mention anymore in your letters about gold; and sorry enough I am that ever since a thought entered into my head; but enough of that subject, for I am really sick of it, for had it not been for those ideas, or rather dreams, I never should have gone to Otaheite in search of Pearls, where I very near lost my life."

Abbot must have told Drury about the worrying political situation in Virginia. Drury, as always, was full of advice:

"But for the accomplishment of all these purposes let me recommend it to you to steer very clear of all party affairs – I am not ignorant of the disposition of the Virginians therefore would recommend it to you in a peculiar manner to avoid all disputes either religion or politics – Tumult and disturbances arising either from one or the other are never favourable to Natural History and to carry on your design it is absolutely necessary to look with indifferent eyes on all parties whatever. I mention this because I know how difficult it is in some parts of that continent be a silent spectator and without attachment to one side or the other, mans peacable and quiet disposition being liable to be imputed to him as a crime."[43]

There is no evidence that Dru Drury ever travelled beyond the shores of England – or, indeed, beyond the confines of London, but he had a large circle of friends, many of them in influential political positions, both at home and abroad, and he also corresponded with naturalists in many parts of the world. This being so, he was better placed than might be imagined to give Abbot sound advice. He continues, in his ever-helpful vein:

"Since your departure the Royal Society have come to a resolution making a great figure by getting good collection of Natural History to which end they have wrote to all parts of the world where any speculative men are to be found to collect the various articles of nature for them – if you are do not be surprised. The King of Spain is also entering into natural history and has wrote to all his Governors in the Spanish to send over rarities of the respective countries duplicates of which he has promised to the Royal Society upon condition of them sending him produce of Great Britain in return so that it seems Natural History is making great strides in Europe than ever was known."[44]

No doubt Drury was concerned for his young friend, and was encouraging him to continue in his chosen career despite the unrest. Abbot, however, was losing heart. The New World seemed to be against him: war was in the air, collecting was disappointing, he had lost some pre-

PLATE 18 Golden crowned wren (Kinglet) *Regulus satrapa* Lichtenstein [*Motacilla Regularus*]
Male and female.

Plate size 20 × 40 cm. *Birds of Georgia* (Rothschild bequest), pl. 86

*Golden crowned Wren*

cious cargoes en route to England – survival seemed impossible. To make matters worse, it seemed certain that he was not going to be able to fulfil his promises to naturalists and collectors in England. Some, like Martyn, had paid in advance for their commissions, which, given Abbot's character, would have troubled him. William began to think about moving elsewhere.

He became acquainted with William Goodall, a cousin of Parke Goodall, who had lived in Georgia and wished to return there with his Virginian wife. William sang the praises of Georgia but could not afford the cost of returning.

The fact that Georgia had not joined the other colonies in the fight for independence appealed to Abbot and he decided to leave Virginia and move to Georgia with Goodall, his wife and child, footing the cost of the journey. "I furnished 2 horses & was to bear all our expenses, he & one cart to carry his wife & child & a little negro boy & our baggage."

Drury tried to persuade him otherwise, urging Abbot to move not to Georgia but to Surinam on the northeast coast of South America, and advising him to employ an agent in New York. From Surinam specimens could be sent to New York, whence they could be shipped to England and payments made through the same agent:

"Mr Martin tells me he is apprehensive you will soon remove to some other part of America ... if so let me advise you to go to Surinam this man assures me you may readily live in Surinam, as conveniently as New York or any other city on the continent and may go into the woods without any danger of Men or Beasts. The principal point you must settle is that of a correspondent either at New York or some other place on the continent who can send your collections to London and remit you the returns hence. This you see is a matter of absolutely necessary to establish without which you cannot have any intercourse with your friends here in London."[45]

Cantwell (1961) maintains that Abbot was unready to fight against his king, and that he and other Virginians migrated to Georgia, expecting to remain on neutral ground. Certainly, Abbot did not want to be involved in fighting, and these assumptions may in part be right.

For a second time in his life, Abbot was to embark on a journey to another new and unknown land, leaving friends behind. He had grown fond of Parke Goodall and his wife during the time they had spent together, and parted from them with regret, feeling more depressed than when he left England.

Leaving Virginia in December 1775, Abbot and Goodall were travelling in the depths of winter. On the way they stopped once at the house of an uncle of Goodall's who lived near the Tar River in North Carolina, and stayed for a week. On another occasion the weather conditions grew so severe that they were forced to stay with the ferryman for several days before they could cross the

PLATE 19 Centre: Tree spider or Fishing spider, female *Dolomides tenebrosus* [*Aranea*]
*Taken on the trunk of a tree in Ogechee River Swamp, 5th May. These species makes no Web, but chooses a large hollow tree to live in. In fine weather they come out and rest motionless on the body of the Tree with the Head downwards as does all kinds of spiders when they rest. The largeness of the Abdomen and the Smallness of the ligature that connects it with the Thorax, make it I imagine the easiest posture. They prey on the Insects that they meet with upon the trees, that creeps near them, seizing quickness. If they are disturbed they retire into the hollow immediately. This species also lives in cellers, wells and sometimes may be found on the walls of Houses. The adult ones are not very common, but I have met with one of a size larger than the one in the drawing.*
[An added note of Francillon reads – *this is a male of no. 281*]
Signed *J. Abbot. 1800.*

Plate size 18.1 × 23.5 cm. *Insects of Georgia* (Francillon), XIV, p. [3], pl. 1

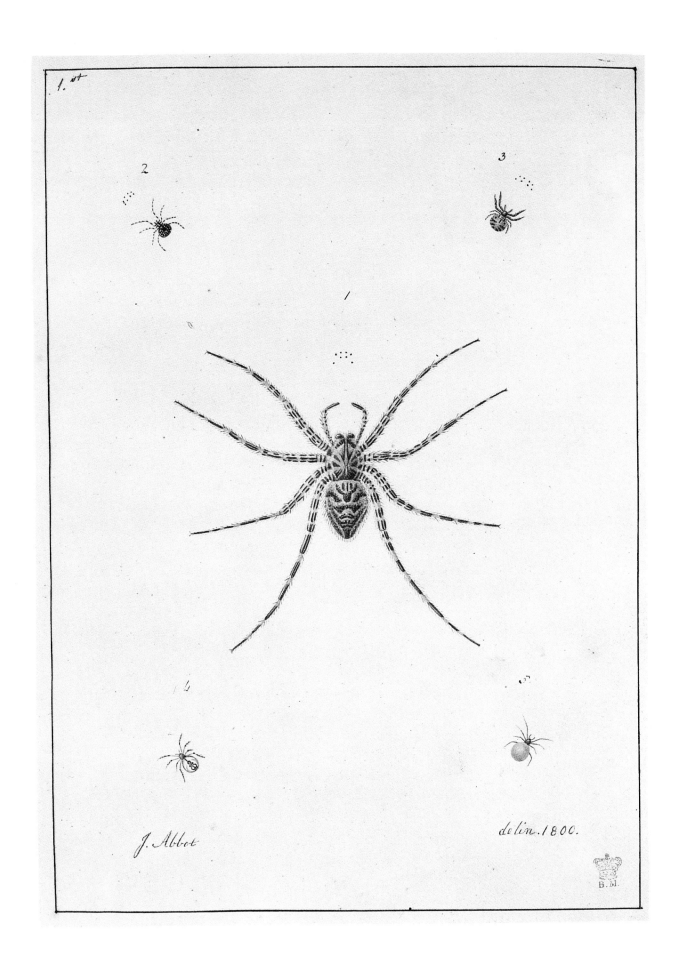

1.st

2

3

1

4

J. Abbot

delin. 1800.

B.M.

45

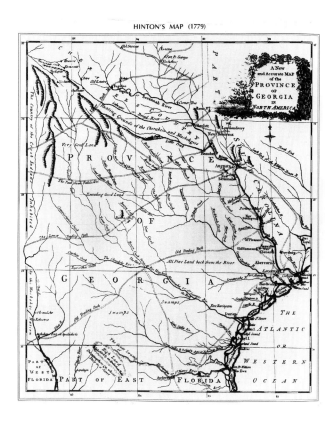

16  Hinton's Map of Georgia, 1779

population in the early 1770s was about 17,000, most of whom lived in small villages and forts on the Atlantic coast and along the Savannah River. The interior was mostly inhabited by Cherokee Indians, whose trails criss-crossed the state and whose economy was mostly sustained by hunting and trading.[47] The little Abbot party may well have used some of the Cherokee trails on their journey south.

"The journey had been completed in about 2 months, in the middle of the winter, but I arrived in good health and spirits, had seen a good deal of the Country, and many amusing passing scenes ... . I was now settled in Georgia for a season I might now take leave of my notes, but as the first years of my living in Georgia, contains much more of Adventure, than the former part of my life, and continued through such bad & terrible time, that I often reflect upon the goodness of providence, in bringing me safely through them."

Promising to continue with them once he is again settled, Abbot brings his 'Notes' to an end; unfortunately for us, they were never completed.

Abbot and his new friends settled some thirty miles south of Augusta, on land next to that owned by William Moore, Goodall's brother-in-law. William Goodall's half-brother, Pleasant, looked after them until a log house for the Goodalls was finished, and they and Abbot could move in. Abbot now embarked, with diligence, on

Roanoke River. At times they made camp in the snow.

The little party finally arrived in Augusta at the beginning of February 1776, some five months before thirteen colonies signed the Declaration of Independence. The State of Georgia (fig. 16) had been granted a charter in 1732 by King George II, when its boundaries included much of present-day Alabama and Mississippi.[46] The

PLATE 20  Spider, female *Araneus saevus* [*Aranea*]

*Fig. 111  Great round Web Spider, these species makes a round web (similar to the English Garden Spider), fastened to trees and bushes and has the same manners with some of the leaves webbed together for a retreat. This is always over the web, whereby they watch the web with their head downwards, it also facilitates their sudden descent upon their prey. All spiders only suck the blood of the larger insects. Taken 25th June, it is not very common, though it is to be met with in the Oak and Pine woods. This species makes a large web, sometimes between two trees.*

*Fig. 112  Aranea. Taken 18th Nov. in the Oakwoods, not very common.*

*Fig. 113  Aranea. Taken 13th May in its web like a garden spider, it is frequent both in the swamps and oak woods.*

*Fig. 114  Aranea. Taken 6th July in the oak woods, not common.*

*Fig. 115  Aranea. Taken 9th July in the oak woods. Not very common.*

Plate size 18.5 × 23 cm. *Insects of Georgia* (Francillon), XIV, p. [25], 23rd drawing (figs. 111–15)

collecting and drawing; he knew he had to work hard to make an adequate living, and there were always going to be delays between his shipments of insects and drawings and the receipt of payments, but he was a disciplined worker who apparently had no difficulty in meeting the demands made upon him.

By the middle of February 1777, Abbot was well established in Georgia, and was living in St George parish of Burke County, north-west of Savannah.[48] That year saw the establishment of the confederate republic of the United States of America, but the war between Britain and the colonists continued. Abbot had moved south to avoid the unrest, but war reached Georgia and skirmishes were commonplace. For most of 1779, Savannah and its surroundings were held by the British. In October of that year, French and American troops laid seige to Savannah and suffered huge losses before retreating. The war ended in 1781, and the British troops eventually left in 1782.[49] In 1802, Georgia ceded to the United States land which was to become Mississippi and Alabama, and the State of Georgia assumed its present form. There is no evidence that Abbot fought;[50] indeed, the indications are that he was strongly pacifist, and by one means or another avoided getting caught up with the military. Presumably, he continued collecting and painting, though he may well have been hampered in this, since even in country areas it was probably extremely dangerous at this time for a man to be seen wandering about collecting insects and sketching – his 'Notes' indicate that his first years in Georgia were dangerous and adventurous times.

Once established in Georgia, and known as a collector, Abbot did get to know other collectors and naturalists, but there are no indications that he wanted to associate himself with any of the formal scientific societies that were being formed in the north – in Philadelphia, Boston and New York – where the study of insect pests for the burgeoning science of agricultural entomology was so important.

In 1727, Benjamin Franklin had laid the foundations for the American Philosophical Society in Philadelphia, which finally got its charter in 1743, with Franklin himself as its first president. Members of the Society included scientists, writers, historians, artisans, merchants and gentleman farmers. During its early years the Society's aims were to promote knowledge and improve practical arts; in later years it centred itself on science. Early society members were particularly interested in natural history, which was to lead on to economic botany and entomology. Boston had its own philosophical society as early as 1683, but it quickly expired, before being revived in 1780 as the American Academy of Arts and Sciences. A main objective was "to promote and encourage knowledge of the antiquities of America and the natural history of the country". The first entomological society – the Entomological Society of Pennsylvania – was founded in 1842, after Abbot's death. It concentrated on the publication of descriptions of new species, and did not initially establish permanent insect collections.

Abbot gradually settled into an ordered life, collecting and breeding his insects and shipping them, and paintings, back to Europe. Customers were expected to supply their own cork-lined boxes, but specimens had to be pinned and packed with meticulous care; damaged specimens were unacceptable and would not be paid for. Abbot became an expert at pinning his specimens in such a way that no damage was sustained during transit, and for this earned a well deserved reputation. If a customer had also requested paintings, his normal habit was to pack them beneath the cork linings; in this way, not only were they fully protected from damage, but also from the prying eyes of custom officials, thus saving his customers further expense from customs duty. The boxes were covered with several layers of packing and finally with a tar-soaked cloth to prevent water entering and spoiling the contents. Most of Abbot's customers required butterflies set with their wings open and flat; some preferred to do this themselves.

Abbot also set up a large breeding programme. Adult specimens were most in demand for customers, but Abbot needed the earlier stages for his illustrations and notes, and he became known for his stuffed caterpillars: "this gentleman was remarkable for the admirable manner in which he prepared caterpillars, so as scarcely to differ from life."[51]

He now began to concentrate on collecting the larval stages of butterflies and moths, which he carefully bred

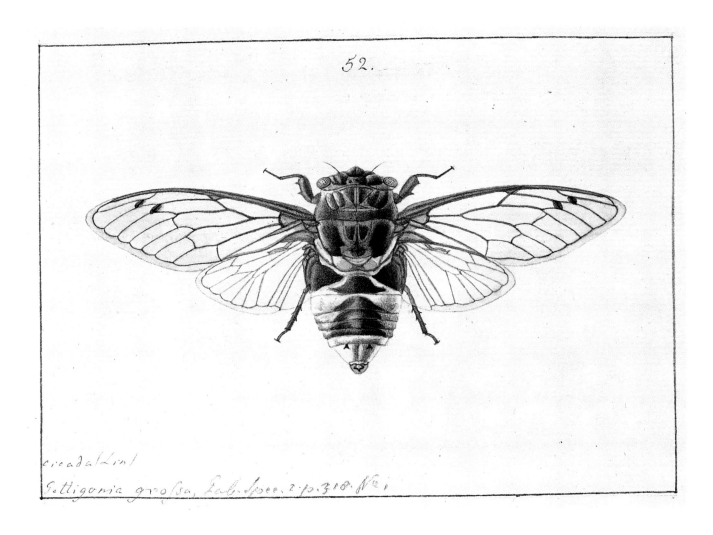

52.

*cicada(Lin)*

*Settigonia grossa, Fab. Spec. 2. p. 318. N. 1.*

PLATE 21  Cicada  *Cicada grossa* Fab.

*Taken 2nd June and as late as November 30th. Common. This genus lives in the Ground in the Caterpillar or Larval state, when full fed they come out of the ground and climb up some Tree or Bush where they shed their skins and come out in the Fly state like the Libellula.*

Plate size 16 × 11 cm. *Insects of Georgia* (Francillon), V, p. [46], pl. 52

so that he could ascertain the association between larvae and the adults – particularly necessary for all the new species that he found. He also made a point of painting them on their food plants, though, by his own admission, he had little knowledge of botany. It was not only the beauty of his paintings and drawings, but the portrayal of the lifecycles of insects and the plants on which they fed that made his paintings so desirable to enthusiasts of entomology.

Abbot's notes were carefully taken. He noted how long it took insects to spin their cocoons, how much time elapsed before the adults emerged, and where they were found. His paintings were annotated with what we would now call ecological notes – comments on life histories and changes that he saw in the countryside. They provided biological information that was previously unknown to his friends and colleagues across the Atlantic, for he was a keen and careful observer who put down everything he saw.

By 1779, John had married a Sarah Warren, and during that year a son was born, and also named John.[52] In 1784, Abbot applied for a headright grant of 200 acres in Burke County, which he eventually received in 1789. Between 1733 and 1909 Georgia used the headright system of land distribution in more settled areas – a system that allowed settlers a certain amount of land with random boundaries "right of a person's head". The 'grant' of surveyed land was given subject to conditions that included a commitment to settle and develop the land. By 1805 distribution by lottery was also introduced for less settled areas.[53] By the time he married he had built and established his own home, but with a wife and son

to support he supplemented his income by doing some teaching. Mr Rice had taught grammar, and Abbot did the same for a short time, probably at Burke County Academy, near Waynesboro. It is also known that he invested some money in a small cotton plantation.[54] Yet, all this time, Abbot continued painting and collecting.

Briar Creek near Savannah was one of his favourite and most convenient collecting areas, but he also collected along the Ogechee (Ogochee) and Savannah Rivers, particularly in the oak woods and swamp areas surrounding that area. Farmers were already draining and planting, causing decreases in the bird populations, and Abbot noted how the ponds in pine woods often became shallow holes in the summer and predicted that some birds would become rare as the country became more settled. Hinton's early map of the area (fig. 16) shows that he must have travelled long distances, probably on horseback, no doubt camping out for several nights, or taking advantage of the hospitality usually offered in the scattered homesteads. Little escaped his notice. He collected the smallest beetle and spider as well as the largest and most exotic-looking butterfly. He diligently walked the river banks and coastal flats collecting aquatic insects and crabs.

Abbot ranged over large areas of Georgia, meticulously recording his observations. He used the port of Savannah to send and receive correspondence, commissions and supplies for his work. Demands for specimens and watercolours came from both Europe and North America.

Before his departure for America, Abbot had formed a business relationship with John Francillon (1744–1816),

PLATE 22  Orange tree butterfly  *Papilio troas* (Linn.) [*Papilio, Equites troas*]
Plant: Orange tree  *Citrus aurantium* (L.)

*The caterpillars feed on the Orange Trees and Prickly Ash. No. 235. It tied itself 6th May and changed into a chrysalis 7th and Bred 27th, another that changed 15th May was bred 3rd June, and another that changed 30th June bred 19th July. It is to be met in Gardens, in the Neighbourhood of Savannah. This species is not common.*

Abbot sold a number of variations of this plate. One identical to this is in a private collection in the USA. Abbot is known to have sent a similar one to his friend Swainson.

Plate size 23 × 30 cm. *Insects of Georgia* (Francillon), XVI, p. [15], pl. 238

who acted as a sort of agent for him. Abbot had armed himself with commissions before he left London, and dealt direct with many friends and correspondents, but Francillon would always take and sell on any additional specimens that Abbot could send him. It was to prove a successful partnership until Francillon's death. Francillon is always described as Abbot's agent, but their financial arrangements are mysterious; profit seems not necessarily to have been the prime consideration. In October 1813, Francillon wrote to William Swainson (see p. 68), offering him 1800 specimens for only £54, including the price of custom clearing and duty: "This is the price I am ordered to sell them for, I don't wish to make any profit upon them, but only to serve my friend."[55]

Francillon received a collection of bird paintings from Abbot in 1792. These he sold to the Trustees of Chethams Library in Manchester for five shillings and sixpence a drawing. He wrote to John Leigh Phillips (see p. 104) in October 1772: "I am extremely obliged to you for your great kindness in selling the Drawings of birds, and I have wrote to Mr Abbot to continue to make all possible additions he can with the Eggs to them ... . I hope you will not take it amiss, as I plead for a poor widow who is much in want at this time, to whom I am ordered by Mr Abbot to pay the money to, as soon as I could sell them." And again in December: "I am infinitely obliged to you for your remittance of £27.0.0 for Mr Abbots 100 drawings of Birds and the woman whom I pay the money to is much obliged likewise to you."[56]

Who is this poor widow that John Abbot was supporting? Did Francillon pay over all the funds that he raised from the sale of Abbot's work in London, or was this a once-only plea for help? It may have been Abbot's mother, but it seems unlikely. Abbot's father had been a wealthy man and his mother and sisters are likely to have been well provided for. This intriguing mystery will only be solved if more of Abbot's papers are discovered.

Like Dru Drury, Francillon was a London jeweller. In spite of Mackechnie-Jarvis (1976) stating that Francillon practised as a physician, *The Gentleman's Magazine* describes him in an obituary as a jeweller of Norfolk Street, Strand. Certainly the correspondence between Francillon and Phillips places him at 24 Norfolk Street.[57] Francillon was also the possessor of a large and enviable collection for which he frequently purchased specimens, and Abbot was a rich source of these specimens. After his death his collection of insects was auctioned at the sale room of Mr King in Covent Garden (fig. 17), when some 72 drawers of insects, many containing specimens from Georgia, were sold. The sale catalogue described the collection as "being undoubtedly the most magnificent cabinet of insects that has ever been brought to sale in this country".[58] However, Francillon did not only deal in Abbot specimens; he also sold on his paintings — and, more importantly, bought huge numbers for himself (see p. 90). It seems probable that he also used these as samples of Abbot's work for prospective purchasers, and was not opposed to lending them to other collectors — in order to help them identify their specimens or, sometimes, to illustrate their own books.[59]

Abbot had proved himself to be a collector and artist of distinction, and his reputation was spreading. His

PLATE 23 Fritillary *Nymphalis phalerati, Agraulis vanillae* (?) [Great American Silver spotted Fritilary Butterfly, *Papilio Passiflora vanilla* of Linn.]
Plant: May cock or May apple or Flesh coloured passion flower *Passiflora incarnata* (Linnaeus)

*The caterpillar feeds on the passion flower called in Georgia Maycock and May Apple* [Modern usage seems to be May pops or May-pop]. *It tyed itself up by the tail 8th July changed into a chrysalis 9th Bred 17th, both caterpillar and butterfly is frequent in most parts of the country.*

Similar to plate 12 in Smith and Abbot 1797. This plate shows how so much superior Abbot's butterflies painted in a natural pose are to those painted with wings outstretched.

Plate size 23 × 30 cm. *Insects of Georgia* (Francillon), XVI, p. [30], pl. 6

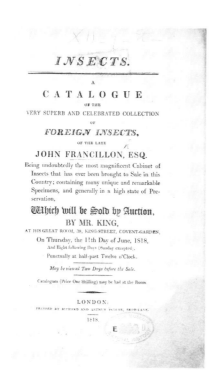

enthusiasm never seemed to wane, and his main occupation in life was to supply his customers with what they required. His income depended on his ability to fulfill these requests, and the reputation he had acquired for the delivery of perfect specimens, together with his beautiful paintings, accompanied by detailed biological notes, ensured a constant stream of requests. At the same time, he was always willing to share his knowledge with others, accompanying visiting collectors to areas that he knew well, and guiding them to where he knew some species to be indigenous.

Abbot's name was also known by now to the American fraternity of naturalists. In 1805, Abbot had met Augustus Gottlieb Oemler (1770–1852), a Savannah pharmacist with a consuming interest in natural history, botany in particular. Oemler had been born in Germany and arrived in America in his early teens. These men with similar interests were to become lifelong friends, and it was Oemler who was responsible for Abbot's later interest in botany.[60]

By the early 1800s, quite large numbers of European books were entering America, but works on natural history seem to have been thin on the ground. Thomas Say (1787–1834) from Philadelphia, a leading naturalist among a small coterie of entomologists in the north, wrote to one of his colleagues expressing his concern over the lack of entomological literature in America.[61] The expense of obtaining such works from abroad was high, and copies that existed were in constant demand to be borrowed and in some cases copied by hand.

17 Francillon sale catalogue, title page and list of Georgia specimens probably collected by Abbot

PLATE 24 Mourning cloak or Camberwell beauty  *Nymphalis antiopa* (L.) [*Papilio Antiopa*]

*Caterpillar feeds on willow; one year I met with a brood of these Caterpillars on a Willow in number near 300, the caterpillar is black frosted with yellow white and spotted with Red. Tyed up by the tail 23rd April, changed into a chrysalis 24th and bred 24th May. This butterfly frequents swamps and low grounds, some years very rare. It lives all through the winter and lays its eggs early in the Spring. Two chrysalids that I pinned soon after they had changed, not withstanding their being pinnd, instead of dying, broke the shell of the chrysalis and would have come out in the butterfly state had they not have been pinned down.*

Upper and underside of butterfly shown.

Plate size 11.5 × 16 cm. *Insects of Georgia* (Francillon), VI, p. [37], pls. 24 and 25

18 Portrait of James Edward Smith (1759–1828), from *The Gentleman's Magazine* (1828), accompanying his obituary

Abbot and Say did not meet; Say, unlike Abbot, was intent on publishing his findings, perhaps hoping that his *American Entomology* (1824) would stand beside Alexander Wilson's *American Ornithology* (see p. 64). He encouraged the publication by American naturalists of material about American species, seeing this as a way to increase the prestige of entomology in the New World. Say did not look with favour on his colleague Le Conte when he took his huge collection of beetles to Paris for the French entomologist Dejean to describe, nor when he discovered that Abbot had been employed by Le Conte to prepare the illustrations for his work on the American lepidoptera, and that it, too, was to be published in Paris, with the French naturalist Boisduval as co-author (see

pp. 96–98).

It might have been expected that Abbot would embark on publication on his own account, but he remained a supplier of illustrations for other authors – and one who was rarely acknowledged. Only one work was to carry his name, and that as joint author. In 1797, James Edward Smith (1759–1828) (fig. 18) published a work in two volumes, entitled *The Natural History of the rarer Lepidopterous Insects of Georgia*. Smith was president of the Linnean Society in London, and knew Abbot's paintings of insects well. Linnaeus's widow had sold her husband's scientific collections and library to Smith; he, with others, had founded the Linnean Society in 1788. One hundred and four of Abbot's watercolours, reproduced as hand-coloured engravings, feature in Smith's work, many being the first published reference to the species described. Abbot's name appears on the title page and Smith readily acknowledges Abbot's information on habitats, his biological notes, and other data found in the annotations to his paintings:

"The materials of the following work have been collected on the spot by the faithful observer Mr John Abbot, many years resident in Georgia. The result of his observations he had delineated in a style of beauty and accuracy which can scarcely be excelled – and has accompanied his figures with an account, as well as a representation. For all such facts recorded in these pages the public are entirely obliged to Mr. Abbot."[62]

Smith was generous with his comments on Abbot's work. In the introduction to the second volume he explained why he considered Abbot's work superior to that of others who had gone before him:

"The splendid works of Clerck, Cramer and Olivier,

PLATE 25 [*Papilio orithya* var.]

*The caterpillar tyed itself up by the tail 16 April, changed into a chrysalis 18th bred 4th May. Comes out again in the autumn a second brood. Common, called in Savannah American Peacock Butterfly.*
Upper and underside of butterfly shown.

Plate size 10.3 × 15 cm. *Insects of Georgia* (Francillon), VI, p. [30], pls. 30 and 31

31

*Orithya var:*

This seems most like one in Cram L. 290. C.D. but is strictly like none
yet figured – compare Pl. 203. C.D. – & 286. E, F besides those
quoted in Fabr.

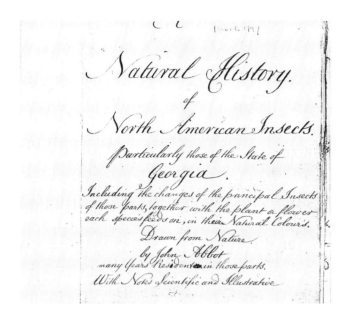

19 Title page of Abbot manuscript for *Natural History of North American Insects*, published as *The Natural History of the rarer Lepidopterous Insects of Georgia* (1797), sent to J.E. Smith, Linnean Society, London

and the more exquisite one of Drury, do indeed display the complete insect in a degree of perfection that leaves scarcely anything to be desired — but where are the metamorphoses through which these finished forms have passed? and where are their various habitation, food, and manners?"[63]

This was the only work to bear Abbot's name, and some maintain that it was many years before Abbot knew of it, with Smith possibly buying or borrowing the plates from Francillon. This was not so. The Archives of the Linnean Society contain the Abbot manuscript sent to Smith (fig. 19):

"A natural history of North American insects — particularly those of the State of Georgia including the changes of the principal insects of those parts, together

with the plant or flower each species feeds on, in their natural colours ... Drawn from nature by John Abbot many years resident in those parts with notes on scientific and illustrative.

"As I intend the following, I think you may publish it as a separate work from any other you are engaged in. However, if you think otherwise you may only mention my name now and then. As we are all naturally fond, as my Lord Bolingbroke observed of recording and immortalizing our great works You may therefore, prune and trim what you please of the following rude notes I shall therefore, not marshal them in any order take them as they occur. I have not pretended to describe them in any scientific manner; leaving that for your superior abilities; nor yet their colours, but only what you could be informed otherwise."[64]

There are ten pages of these notes, giving general information on butterflies and moths and caterpillars. Some of these notes have been annotated, probably by Smith, to correct some of the style, and as Abbot directed, "to prune and trim and marshall in his own order" (fig. 20).

It is evident that, even so far from London, Abbot was in touch with the London scientific circle. He knew Smith well and knew that he had published other works. There are no papers to indicate whether Smith was instrumental in directly requesting the paintings and observations from Abbot, or whether Abbot wrote to him suggesting the publication; the latter seems likely. The work was published with both English and French texts, as was usual for the time, and was the first important publication on American entomology. It seems unlikely that Smith would have neglected to send Abbot a copy (fig. 21).

James Edwards (1757–1816) was the printer and pub-

PLATE 26 [*Papilio c. aureum*]

*The caterpillar black, brown and orange. feeds on Elm and Sugar Berry, most frequent in Ogochee Swamps, it tyed itself up by the tail 29th May, changed into a chrysalis 30th bred 7th June. The Butterfly sucks damp open Ground, not very common, called in Savannah American Common Butterfly.*
Upper and underside of butterfly shown.

Plate size 10 × 15 cm. *Insects of Georgia* (Francillon), VI, p. [39], pls. 26 and 27

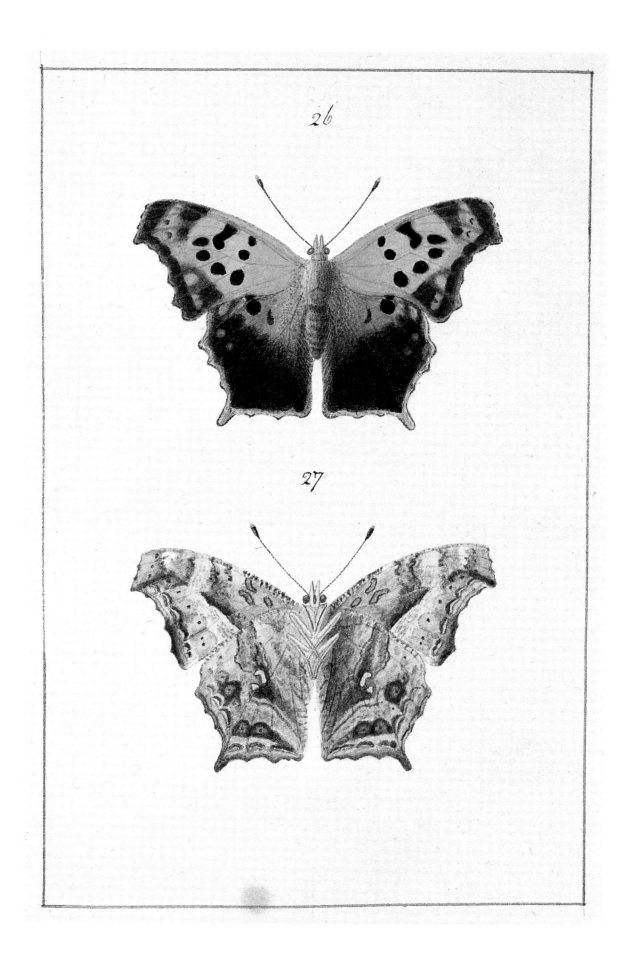

20 Introduction and sample page showing Smith's corrections to Abbot's manuscript, Linnean Society, London

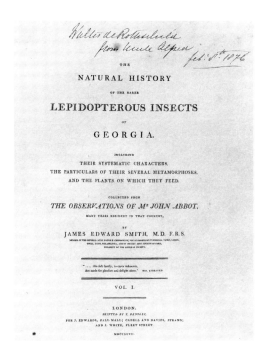

21 *The Natural History of the rarer Lepidopterous Insects of Georgia*, vol. 1 (1797), title page

lisher of this magnificent work, which was well received but was not a financial success. Smith dedicated the work to Mariamne Johnes (1748–1811), a young friend who had an impressive knowledge of natural history. The copy he sent her contained Abbot's originals. A letter from her father was also included: "Mr Edwards has just given you the most magnificent and beautiful present I have seen – nothing less than the original drawings of the American insects."

Abbot believed himself unqualified to name the specimens that he drew, but sought perfect accuracy in his paintings so that every specimen could be identified or described by others more able than he. He was acutely aware that the colours of the specimens often faded as they dried, and with this in mind he tried to match the

PLATE 27   ?*Eurytides marcellus* Cramer [*Ajax*]

*Papilio Ajax. Frequents blossoms. Flies very swift, Caterpillar green marked with black, feeds on the Papaw. Changed into chrysalis 24th May, Bred 16th June. One that changed in Autumn was bred 2nd March. Not very common. Called in Savannah Black and White barred Swallow tailed Butterfly. 15. Underside.*

Plate size 11.5 × 16.5 cm. *Insects of Georgia* (Francillon), VI, p. [10], pls. 14 and 15

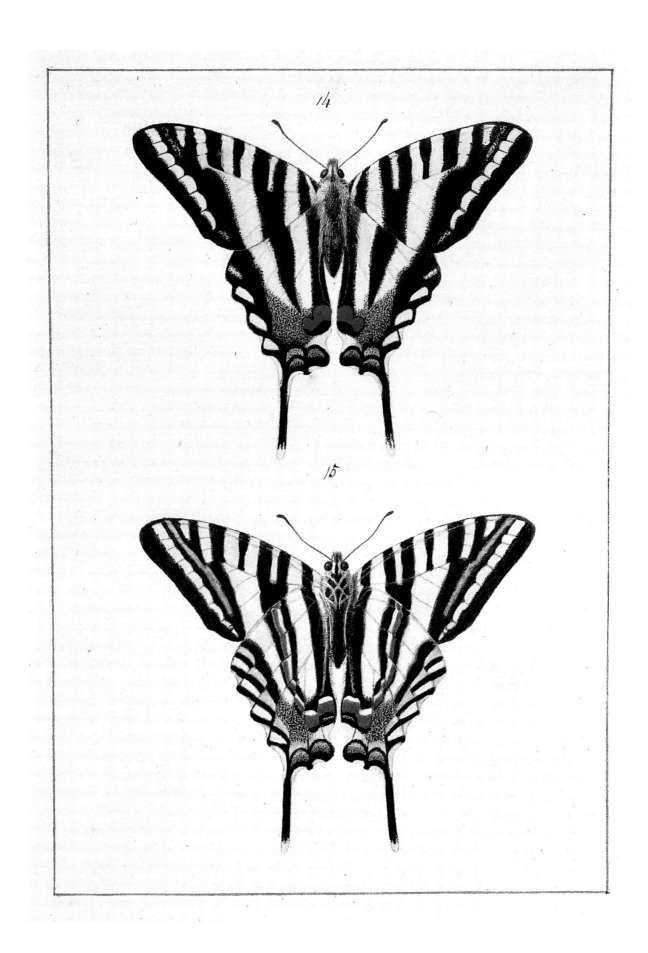

22  Portrait of John Latham (1740–1837)

in 1791, and sent to Francillon in London. These paintings were the first of many hundreds to be bought by private collectors and by the authors of ornithological works. As ever, Abbot was content to leave the task of authorship to others. Had he ventured into the sphere of scholarly publication, as many of his contemporaries did, his beautiful and accurate illustrations and first-hand observations on breeding and habitats would have preceded those of such early ornithological authors as John James Audubon (1785–1851) and Abbot's friend and fellow artist, Alexander Wilson (see p. 64). As it is, Abbot's paintings are among the earliest representations of the avifauna of North America. Simpson (1984) establishes Abbot as the real pioneer of American ornithology, describing him as a biological illustrator of exceptional talent.

Abbot had been collecting birds and preparing their skins for customers well before he began illustrating them. John Latham (1740–1837) (fig. 22), author of *General Synopsis of Birds* and of two supplements to this work (1781–85), refers to specimens in the "collections of Mr Humphries",[65] and in Supplement II (1801) says that these specimens "came from several miles within South Georgia". Abbot is not mentioned by name, but Abbot had worked for Humphries [Humphrey] before leaving London and is the only naturalist known to have been collecting in Georgia at such an early date. However, Latham seems also to have been in direct contact with Abbot, for in the same supplement he acknowledges information received from Abbot, and one can only suppose that an enthusiast such as Latham would have prevailed upon Abbot to send him specimens. In 1809, Latham saw but did not buy a large consignment of bird specimens that had arrived in London for Francillon (see p. 104). Sixty-four of these specimens were, however, bought by Lord Stanley and incorporated into his collections at Knowsley Hall, Liverpool.

tints of his watercolours as accurately as possible to live or freshly killed specimens.

The popularity of Abbot's paintings and drawings lay partly in the accuracy of the representations but also in the inclusion of the metamorphosis of the insects that he portrayed, and the addition of their food plants, which he always included. Abbot was not the first to do this. The gifted seventeenth-century Dutch entomologist Maria Sibylla Merian (1647–1717) had done this in her *Der Raupen wunderbare Verwandelung* (1679–83), and more particularly in *Metamorphosis Insectorum Surinamensium* (1705). The style of these works is considerably more extravagant than that of Abbot, but Abbot would surely have known and been influenced by Merian's books. If he did not own copies of them, he would certainly have seen them at the home of his friend and mentor; Drury's sale catalogue shows he had them in his library.

Abbot's first love was insects, but he was ready to collect and draw other species that were requested of him. The earliest set of Abbot's bird illustrations was completed

Abbot's collecting of birds was every bit as meticu-

PLATE 28  *Pterourous troilus* Cramer [*Troilus*]

*Papilio Troilus. Taken 10th March sucking wet and damp places in yards and edges of water in open grounds.*
*Called in Savannah Black Sassafrass Swallowtailed Butterfly. 8. Underside.*

Plate size 12.5 × 17.5 cm. *Insects of Georgia* (Francillon), VI, p. [3], pls. 7 and 8

7

8

lous as that of his insects. Specimens were carefully prepared and knowledgeably annotated from his own careful observations, to provide scientific data for the publications of his customers. However, as his bird collecting increased, Abbot had problems preserving his specimens. He had made friends with another English naturalist, William Swainson (see p. 68), and, knowing that Swainson had collected birds in South America, wrote to him asking if he had any remedies:

"1818 Bullock County, Georgia
... I have failed in every method hitherto to preserve them, every poison that I have tried being insufficient, except the bird or insect could be entirely soaked in any poison, which would then destroy its colours."[66]

Swainson replies in the same year:

"... I will put you in possession of a receipt for both which has enabled me to bring the whole of my collections home in the most perfect state not withstanding all the destructive little insects found in South America. It is indeed invaluable, as was, if known might save entire Museums from decay, but I believe the secret rests with me."

A fairly lethal recipe follows, containing potash, quicklime, camphor and grated soap – and with a warning to use it with care!

"... to prevent the least drop getting under the nails, as it will separate the nails from the skin, and cause some pain, but this is easily prevented by washing the hands immediately after finishing each bird."[67]

In 1809, Abbot met the American ornithologist Alexander Wilson (1766–1831). Wilson, the 'father of American ornithology', had come to America from Scotland, and had embarked on a multi-volume work, *American Ornithology* (1808–13), the first and most important work on American birds. Abbot and Wilson travelled together on several collecting excursions and Abbot was to prove invaluable to Wilson, providing him with many specimens and paintings for his books. Abbot's detailed information on localities and habitats of birds made a huge contribution to the success of *American Ornithology*. In March 1809, Wilson wrote from Savannah to his naturalist friend William Bartram: "There is a Mr Abbot here, who has resided in Georgia thirty-three years, drawing insects and birds. I have been on several excursions with him. He is a good observer and paints well".[68]

It was a bird lover, Joseph Prentice, a subscriber to Wilson's *American Ornithology* and a provider of ornithological information to the author, who had introduced Wilson to "an unknown authority on Southern Birds". Prentice had convinced Wilson that no one could possibly know more about birds of his region than Abbot. Wilson was not to be disappointed. Abbot took him to many of the best collecting places, and was able to identify birds which Wilson was not sure about. Wilson was amazed by this "mysteriously modest and obliging" man who had such an extensive knowledge of birds, their habitats and their biology, and an artistic ability that was perhaps (though Wilson admitted this only to himself) superior to his own. Wilson was mystified why scientists in Philadelphia had never heard of him.[69]

Abbot continued to send specimens and information to Wilson after he returned home. Knowing what a meticulous observer Abbot was, Wilson could rely on his information. He gave Abbot full credit for his

PLATE 29 [White butterfly *Papilio Danaii candidi*]

*This caterpillar feeds on the plant figures. It tyed itself up 16th July and changed into the chrysalis 17th and bred 23rd. near half the female Butterflies varies being a dingy black as figured. They continue in plenty about Savannah all this last summer but I have rarely seen any for the last twelve years. I am indebted for this discovery of these caterpillars to my friend Mr. Oemler who first found it in his garden in Savannah.*

Plate size 23 × 30 cm. *Insects of Georgia* (Francillon), XV, p. [31], pl. 275

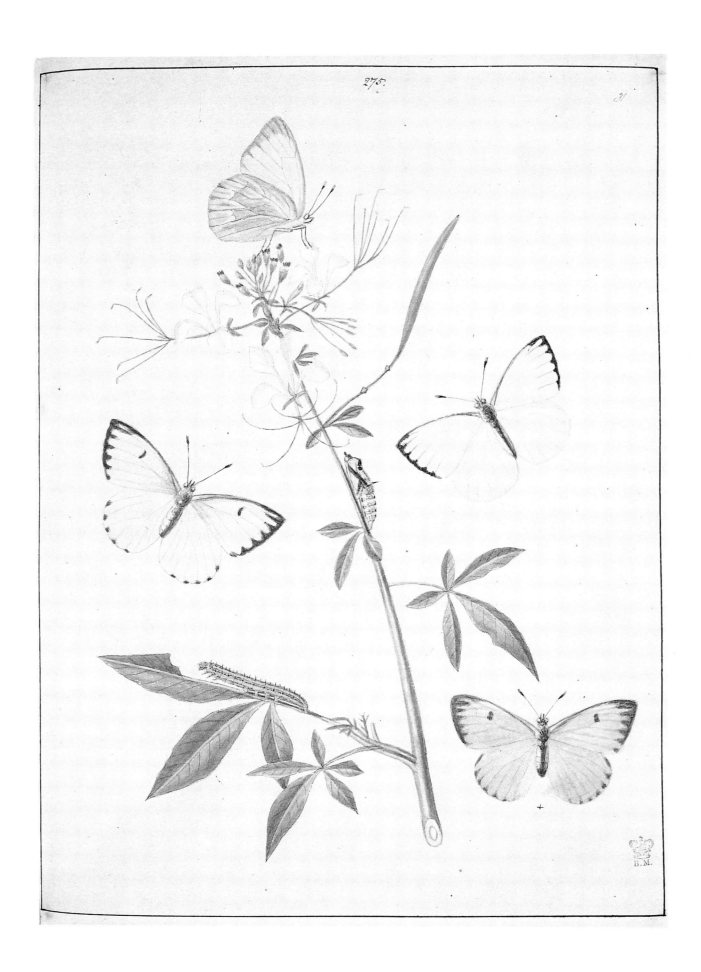

contribution to *American Ornithology* in the books, and was generous with his payments and his praise of Abbot's work: "... he paid the secluded artist the only tribute he ever received, however, in the United States."[70]

In 1812, Wilson wrote to Abbot from his home in Philadelphia:

"Mr John Abbot, Naturalist, Savannah, Georgia
Philad. 23. Jany. 1812.
I this day rec'd a small box containing a roll of Drawings, 3 in number, which I myself delivered to Dr. Barton,[71] also a small package directed to Wm Bartram ... and 4 birds viz., the Small Crow, female solitary Flycatcher and the male and female Ground Dove – all in good order – ... will you please draw on me thro' Mr Oemler for the amount of these 4 and any other you may send. Please send the Chuck Wills Widow (male) and eggs, and the beautiful rare Sparrow you mention, also the Stripped Wren. I do not know the large Green-billed woodpecker – nor any such Woodpecker as large as the Woodcocks – if you know of such, be so good as to send me one ... one large folio of the Lepidopterous insects of Georgia. It is a very splendid work I will send you a list of all the land and waterbirds which I have yet to draw – marking those with a star that I think you can finish me with.

In the meantime, send me by the first opportunity what you can in a strong box directed to A. Wilson care of Bradford and Inskeep, Booksellers, PhiIa. I hope you will soon get quit of that disgusting complaint the Rheumatism."[72]

On Wilson's death, the ornithologist George Ord (1781–1866) took over and completed the final two volumes of *American Ornithology*. Abbot continued to extend the same help with specimens and data, and in return Ord accorded the same courtesy to Abbot as Wilson had done, publicly acknowledging the receipt of information about some of the birds published in the final volume.

In 1812, at the age of sixty-one, Abbot decided to abandon natural history and retire to the country. Abbot had left revolutionary Virginia, hoping for a peaceful existence in Georgia – only to find similar circumstances there. He had survived the Revolution, but when Congress declared war on the British on 18 June 1812, it obviously proved too much. He wrote to George Ord in March 1814:

"The islands of lower country of the southern parts of Georgia is the great rendezvoos of the waterbirds but owing to the unhappiness and other circumstances I have never had the pleasure of visiting it. At the commencement of the war I had undertaken to make a collection of stuffed birds and as complete a collection of drawings of them in colours as I was able for a Gentleman in England – but last fall [1813] in dispair of seeing peace restored, I returned into the country after having made about 200 drawings throwed away a large collection of stuffed skins. I have entirely laid it aside, and entered into another line of employment, where I am in hopes the mad and destructive ambition of the rulers of the world can but little interfere."[73]

However, his desertion from natural history did not last long. His "other line of employment" referred to in this letter to Ord is a mystery, and in 1813 he was persuaded by Oemler and Le Conte to return to his beloved work as collector and artist. In 1817, he even added the collection of herbarium specimens for a neighbour to his other activities. Stephen Elliott (1771–1830) had a plantation on the Ogechee River, an area that Abbot

PLATE 30 [Large Yellow spotted black swallow tail butterfly *Papilio Equites Troes*] Plant: Magnolia

*Caterpillar feeds on the Bay (as figured) tyed itself up 30th May, changed into chrysalis 31st. Bred 14th June. Another tyed itself up 17th September. changed 18th. The caterpillar is not common but the butterfly is frequent all over the country but I believe it is not found in the northward states.*

Plate size 23 × 30 cm. *Insects of Georgia* (Francillon), XVI, p. [18], pl. 2

23 Portrait of William Swainson (1789–1855)

specimens to Elliott's herbarium, and some of these Abbot specimens still exist in the Charleston Museum, South Carolina.

Plant collecting was well established – both live plants and herbaria specimens – and Abbot took to it with ease. Inevitably, further botanical requests were to follow, once Abbot's care and abilities in this new sphere were recognized. The gardens created around the great houses of the English aristocracy in the eighteenth century had relied on plant collectors such as Peter Collinson (see p. 24), and owners were willing to pay handsome sums of money for their plants. A Fellow of the Royal Society, Collinson and fellow botanist John Ellis (*ca.* 1705–1766) had done much to encourage and promote the natural sciences in both England and the colonies. Abbot had taken to America Ellis's *The Method of Catching and Preserving Insects for Collections*, a supplement to his larger work *Directions for bringing over Seeds and Plants from the East Indies and other distant countries in a state of vegetation* (1771).

Abbot was a good correspondent and kept in touch with naturalists in other parts of America as well as in England and Europe. Few of his papers have survived, but some items of correspondence still exist in archive collections of those to whom he wrote. The Francillon papers should have been a rich source of Abbot correspondence – but these, with few exceptions, have also disappeared. Although Abbot sold specimens and paintings through Francillon, he also dealt directly with naturalists and collectors, and was diligent in keeping up these contacts, particularly after Francillon's death. One correspondent was the English naturalist William Swainson (1789–1855) (fig. 23).

Swainson, like other naturalists before him, had developed a passion for collecting at an early age. He was particularly keen to collect in the tropics and, in 1815,

covered extensively in his collecting. The American botanist William Baldwin (see p. 74), writing to Abbot, described Elliott as "that excellent Botanist and Entomologist Stephen Elliott Esq. He is like yourself indefatigable; has seen and examined a great many Plants, Minerals and Insects …". Elliott was a businessman and a founder of the Medical College of South Carolina; he had amassed a large insect collection and herbarium, and he and Abbot often exchanged specimens. Probably they collected together and met socially, since their homes were not far apart. Abbot contributed many plant

PLATE 31 Blue butterfly, probably *Calestrina argeolus* (Cramer) [Holly Blue, *Papilio argeolus, Plebeji rurialis*]
Plant: *Erythrina herbacea* [Coral bean]

*The caterpillar feeds on wild kinds of bean figured, Holly etc. It spun or tyed itself up 30th April, changed into a chrysalis 2 May, bred 12th March following. The caterpillar is rare and the butterfly is not common, but it is more frequent in the Hammocks and near swamps.*

Plate size 23 × 30 cm. *Insects of Georgia* (Francillon), XVI, p. [57], pl. 212

after receiving an inheritance, was able to make a trip to South America, returning a year later with hundreds of birds and plants and some 20,000 insects. The sale of part of his collection helped to pay for his trip, but he also wanted to exchange his specimens for ones from other parts of the world, including North America. His first attempt to obtain Abbot specimens from Georgia, however, was not fruitful. He approached Francillon to obtain a collection of insects and was offered two boxes containing some 1800 specimens: "... there are about 1,800 large and small together at 6 pence each £45, and two double cork boxes £3.3.0. Likewise the duty and custom house expenses £5.17.0d. altogether £54.0.0."

Swainson was not enthusiastic about buying specimens he had not specifically commissioned, and asked Francillon to request Abbot to send males and females of rare species. Francillon replied that he would neither want nor be able to return the specimens to Abbot if Swainson was not satisfied, and informed Swainson that he had always been happy with the collections arriving from America. Swainson eventually approached Abbot direct and obtained from him many specimens and a series of watercolours that had been intended as illustrations for a third (unpublished) volume of *The Natural History of the rarer Lepidopterous Insects of Georgia* (see p. 100).

It is difficult to decide who benefited most from the Abbot and Swainson relationship. Swainson was, of course, no dilettante. He wanted to be introduced to useful contacts in order to find a market for his own specimens from South America, and hoped also to obtain insects, birds and plants from Abbot; Abbot in turn was anxious to sell his wares.

The Abbot-Swainson correspondence, held in the archives of the Linnean Society, London, is revealing.

Abbot to Swainson 20 December 1816:

"I lately disposed of a large collection of insects together with most of my drawings I had by me to a gentleman merchant of New York who has now gone back to his native country Switzerland.[74]

"I have commenced making a set of quarto (large size) drawings of the changes of insects of insects with notes, of such insects that are not figured in Smith's Lepidopterous insects of Georgia. At present I am under no particular engagements to any person to collect and draw for, but only Mr Le Conte a gentleman who has a plantation in Georgia ... he has a taste in General natural history ... . Don't you know some friend that would be desirous to have the Coleoptera insects and all Phalinia as I shall still breed and collect them."[75]

Several letters continue this correspondence, giving a good insight into Abbot's activities over a period of some five years.[76]

Abbot wrote to Swainson, 15 January 1820:

"After writing my last letter, I returned home and immediately packed my birds in 3 boxes, amounting upwards of 300 specimens, together with my insects in another containing upwards of 1,000, and brought them to Savannah and unfortunately kept them, at my friends Mr Oemler until I could ship them to you. I was woked out of my first sleep on the night of the 10th by the alarm of a most terrible fire, which aided by a most violent winds and other unfortunate circumstances, spread with irresistible fury and continued until it consumed the entire centre and most of the opulent trading part of the city. The loss of property is immense – my worthy friend Mr. Oemler lost all his collections of Natural History and what is worse nearly all his property. I lost my boxes and some drawings and other person for whom

PLATE 32  Large black-veined orange butterfly  *Basilarchia archippus* (Cramer)? [*Papilio Archippus*]
Plant: Curassavian swallow wort or Butterfly weed [*Asclepias curassavica* L.]

*The caterpillar feeds on the butterfly weed, and the milkey [sic] Pusley [Portulaca oleracea L.] it tyed itself up by the tail 24th April changed into a chrysalis 25h, Bred 11th May another that changed into chrysalis 12 May bred 22nd. It is frequent in this country and likewise in the Northward States.*

Plate size 23 × 30 cm. *Insects of Georgia* (Francillon), XVI, p. [26], pl. 108

24 Collecting insects, from Anon, *History of Insects* (1842)

I should have received payment of a sum of money is also a considerable sufferer so I have little or not hope of receipt of it ... .

But dear Sir, tho' much depressed in spirits I suppose I must not give up to despair – I will with a blessing go home, and begin again to collect."[77]

Thousands of insects and hundreds of birds that he had collected were lost, either at sea or by fire, during Abbot's life, yet he never gave up. His fertile mind made him ever ready to start on something new.

Abbot was a walking encyclopedia of the flora and fauna for miles around his home, generous with information, able to guide collectors to reliable collecting grounds, and knowing exactly where and when to find particular specimens to fulfill specific requests from both American and European clients. Visitors found hospitality in his home and could at the same time view his pattern volumes of paintings. His reputation can be judged by the numbers of collectors who acquired his specimens and paintings, or who sought him out in the hope of visiting his collecting sites and obtaining specimens and paintings of both birds and insects.

John Lyon, a nurseryman and plant hunter had sought out Abbot during his travels in Georgia:

"... got to Briar Creek and three quarters of a mile from the Bridge turned right to call on Mr John Abbot, a curious collector of insects, birds etc., who entertained me very agreeably for several hours in viewing his elegant masterly drawings."[78]

An American nurseryman and botanical collector,

PLATE 33 Trumpet leaf moths. Lower moth   *Tarachidia semiflava* (Guenée)
Upper moth Noctuae   *Phytometra ernestiana* (Blanchard)
Plant: Pitcher plant *Sarracenia* sp.

*The caterpillar feeds on the trumpet leaf. It spun up in the leaf in the hollow part 12th June. Bred 24th. The Moth may also be found sometime in the hollow of the leaf and it flies in the evening. It is Rare. Many insects of different classes creep into the hollow of the leaves for shelter where they drowned by rains filling the hollow of the leaf, as they are unable to get out again from the wet and the shape of the leaf. The drowned insects afford food for a Maggot to a Fly which lays its Eggs there, which I believe is probably near akin to the flesh Flies.*

Plate size 23 × 30 cm. *Insects of Georgia* (Francillon), XVII, p. [91], pl. 156

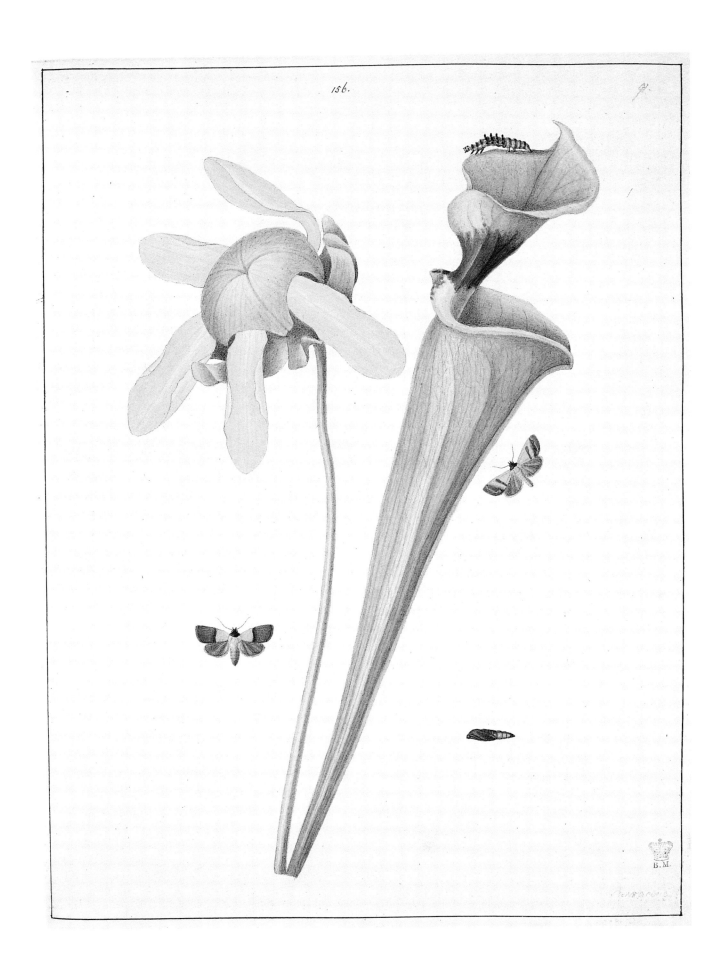

Robert Squib (*fl.* 1780–1806), made several excursions with John Abbot for plants for his herbarium, and no doubt for nursery specimens, and a Lucius Mutton collected bird specimens with Abbot, sharing Abbot's enthusiasm for collecting, observing and drawing birds.

The American botanist William Baldwin (1779–1819), a governor of the Savannah Library Society, was a frequent visitor. In 1811 he wrote to Dr Henry Mühlenberg, a plant collector and enthusiastic botanist who corresponded with Baldwin, wishing to exchange plant specimens: "I have looked over with great pleasure, the interesting drawings of the amiable Mr Abbott. Those at the library ... executed under the inspection of Mr Oemler. They are, as far as I am qualified for judging, exquisitely beautiful and scientifically accurate."[79]

Heinrich Escher-Zollikofer (1776–1853), a Swiss merchant residing in New York, was an enthusiastic collector of Abbot's specimens and paintings – both for his own collections (one of which included some 120 bird skins) and for those of collectors in Europe. He in turn recommended Abbot's diligent and careful collecting to the French ornithologist Frédéric de La Fresnaye (1783–1861). Noël Frédéric Armand André, Baron de La Fresnaye, was an ardent acquirer of natural history specimens, particularly of birds. In 1827, he bought specimens prepared by Abbot, mostly through Heinrich Escher, and the skins in his collection (which was eventually transferred to the Museum of Comparative Zoology at Harvard) are attributed to Abbot of "Savanha". A note bound in The Natural History Museum's copy of *Catalogue des ouvrages scientifiques composant la bibliothèque de M. de La Fresnay* reads: "birds purchased in 1865 by Dr Henry Bryant –

presented to Boston Natural History Society".

In 1811, Friedrich Wilhelm Sieber (1789–1844), who had spent about ten years in Brazil, collecting natural history specimens for Count von Hoffmansegg, returned to Europe. On his way home he passed through London, obtaining some North American specimens in exchange for his own. It seems likely that these were Abbot specimens, and the transaction would presumably have been executed through Francillon. The specimens were deposited in the Zoological Museum in Berlin, but were mostly destroyed during the bombing of World War II.[80]

From time to time Abbot also met collectors from Europe. Prince Maurice-Joseph of Lichtenstein (1775–1819) sent his botanical collector, Aloysius Ensten (*fl.* 1800–10), to Georgia to obtain specimens for his herbarium. Ensten made a point of visiting Abbot, who was able to introduce him to areas likely to yield interesting specimens.

Although Abbot never returned to England, he remained in contact with his family. He told Oemler that he had had no news of his brother, Thomas, since the end of the War of American Independence, but that Thomas "was put as a clerk to an Attorney, and as I heard was a promising young man". His father had died in 1787; perhaps there had been a small inheritance either for himself or for his son.

Abbot's wife, two years older than Abbot, died in November 1817, aged 68. This left Abbot depressed, but he soon got back to his usual routines. His son, John Jnr, is described by Bassett (1938) as a merchant, a trader of slaves and an attorney. Perhaps his father had persuaded him into his grandfather's profession, hoping

PLATE 34  Green swallow-tailed emperor moth  *Actias luna* (L.) [*Bombyx luna*]
Plant:  *Liquidambar styraciflua* L. [Liquid amber or sweet gum]

*The caterpillar feeds on sweet gum, Walnut, Hickory and Persimmon. It spun up in the leaves in a thinner and more irregular web than the former no. 25 [Peacock emperor moth – not shown here], 31st May. The moth came out of the chrysalis 18th June another that spun up on 6th September was bred 5th April, But I have met with the Moth (some Springs) as early as 4th March. Those that breed on Hickory seem to be a variety, the caterpillar is without spots, and the Moth much paler in color. It is also frequent in the Northward States.*

Similar to plate 48 in Smith and Abbot 1797, Vol. 1. The published plate has no fruit.

Plate size 23.5 × 30 cm. *Insects of Georgia* (Francillon), XVI, p. [90], pl. 26

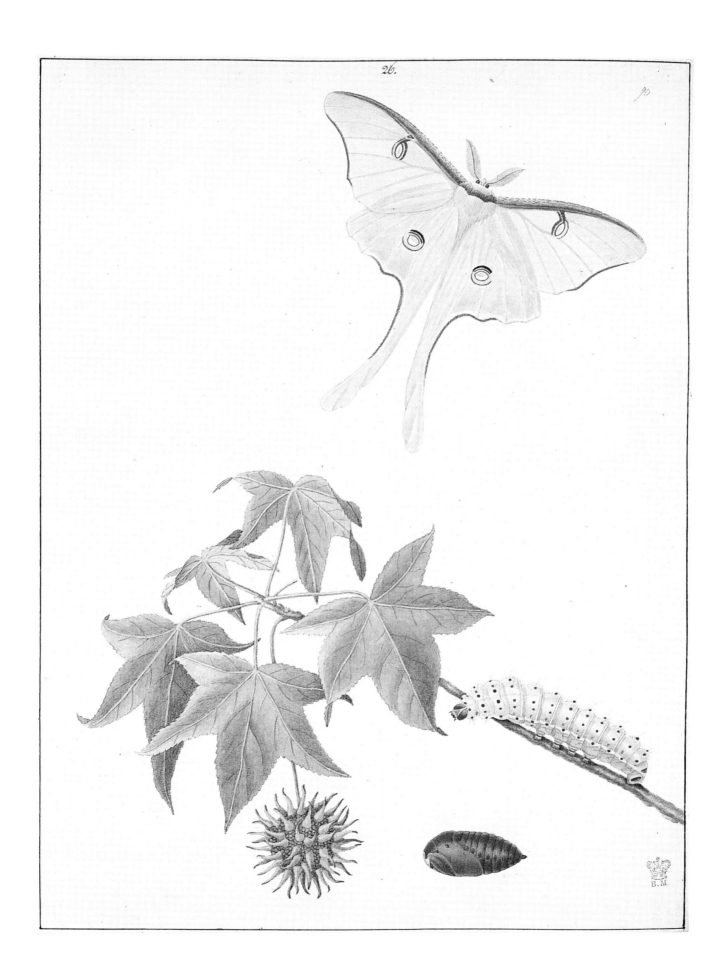

25 Portrait of Thaddeus William Harris
(1795–1856)

Abbot went on collecting and painting into extreme old age. In 1835 (he was then eighty-four) he wrote to Swainson: "I have now sent to you with the letter a box containing 11 small boxes containing 670 insects and about 650 drawings of single insects."[82]

The writing is as firm and sure as it was when he was a much younger man, but colleagues were beginning to speculate that Abbot was giving up or was past his best. In 1834 Abbot had sent a collection of insects to one of his American entomological correspondents, Thaddeus William Harris (1795–1856) (fig. 25) who, with Oemler, had been trying to get greater credit for Abbot and his major contribution to Smith's *Natural History of the rarer Lepidopterous Insects of Georgia*, but with little success. Harris had told Oemler that he had heard that the old man was now blind and being financially supported by Major Le Conte (see p. 96). Oemler puts him to rights:

"... you are under the impression that the old man was now blind and solely supported by Major Le Conte Mr. Abbot has used glasses ever since I have known him, (1805) and – by means of them paints the smallest insects with pretty much correctness ... As for to be supported by Major Le Conte that is not so – a petty allowance of six and a quarter cents for the drawing of an insect."[83]

The tone of the letter suggests that Oemler felt that his old friend Abbot was being insulted, and he was quick to defend him. Abbot also wrote to Harris in 1835:

"In reply to your request at what price I sell my collections of Insects, my usual price is 6 dollars per hundred large and small, rare and common. My charge to Mr Le Conte for my drawings and for whom I continue to draw for every year the size of which I have figured at the end

that it would be lucrative for his son in the New World. He is said to have had a business trading under the name of John Abbot Fur Company. In 1808, he defaulted on his taxes and his business was dissolved. In April 1812, he married Eliza Rawls, and a year later bought a property, which was eventually mortgaged to secure a very large debt. The mortgage was paid – presumably by his father – and, in 1819, Abbot senior was a witness at the trial of his son for debt. There is some suggestion that Abbot brought about his own financial ruin by paying off his son's debts. By 1826, John Abbot Jnr had died of a liver complaint. Abbot gave over some slaves to his daughter-in-law, and probably money to help her with living expenses; she seems to have been little support to her father-in-law in his declining years.[81]

PLATE 35  Pine sphinx  *Lapara coniferarum* L. [*Sphinx pinus coniferarum*]
Plant: Long-leaf pine  *Pinus palustris* (Mill.)

*The caterpillar feeds on the long-leaved pine. Pinus palustris, short leaved pine and sometimes Cypress. It went into the ground 16th June, bred 8th April. The moth may at times be found settled on the body of pine Trees in the Woods. It is not common.*

Plate size 23.5 × 30 cm. *Insects of Georgia* (Francillon), XV, p. [77], pl. 308

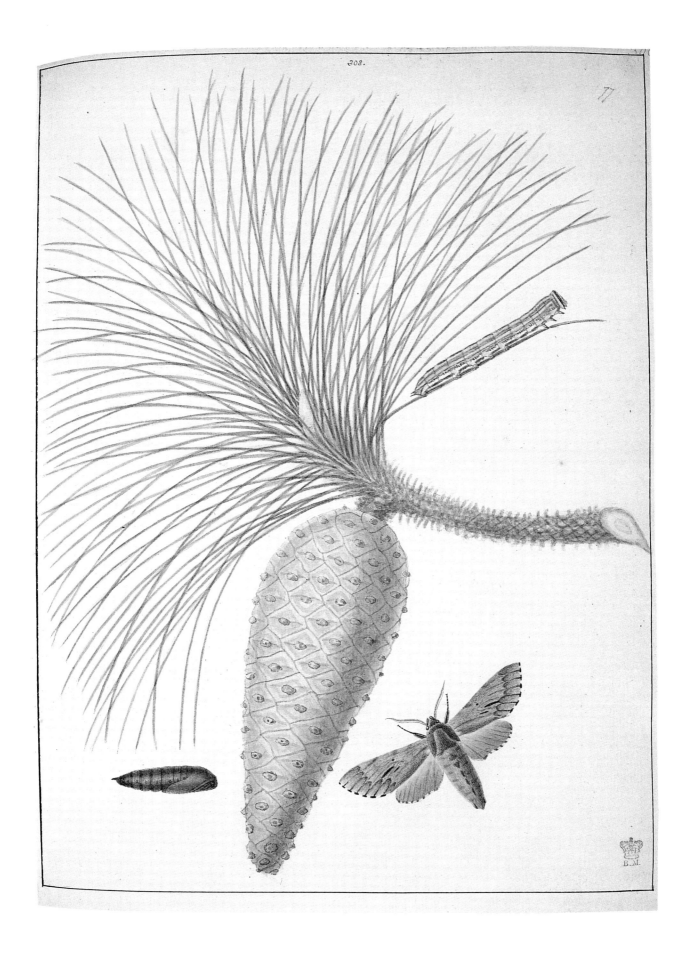

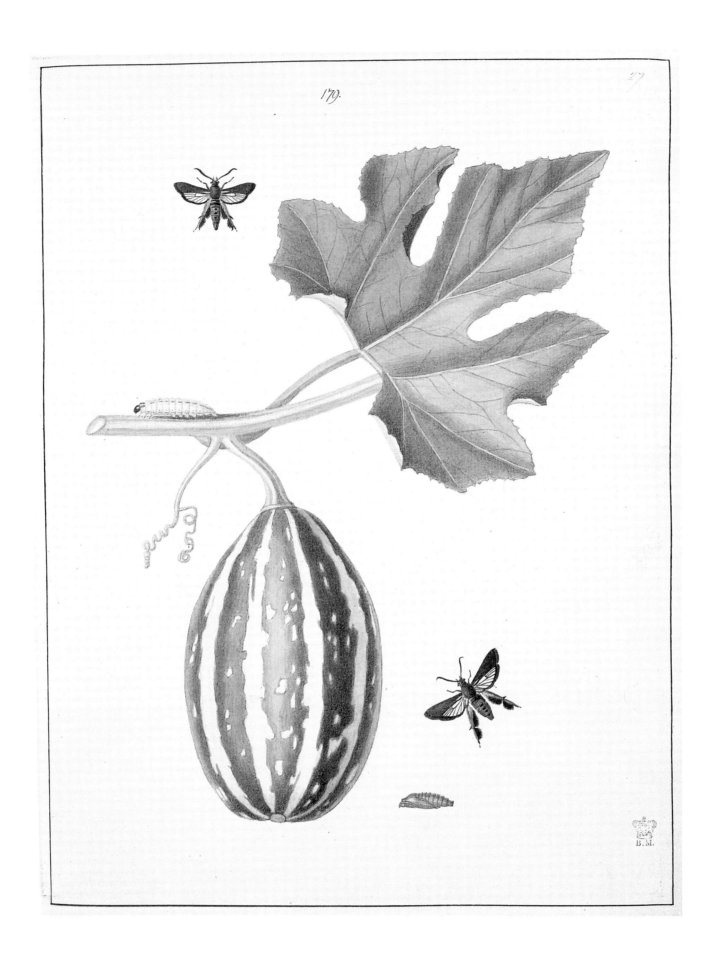

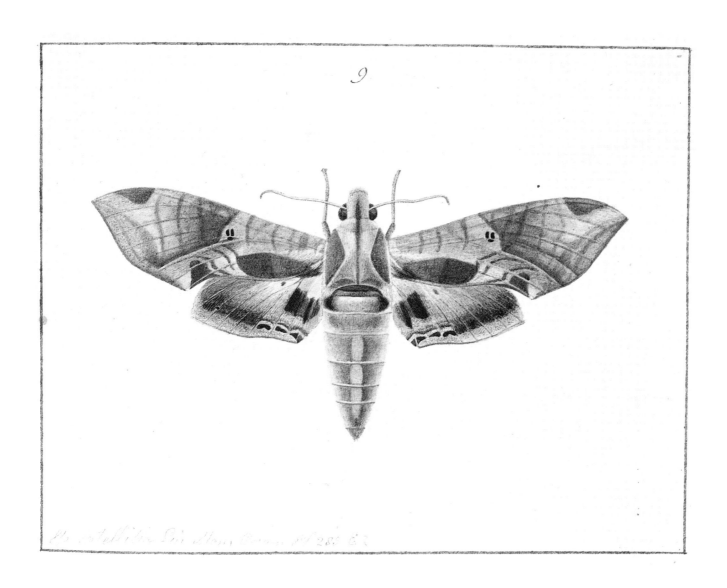

*9*

PLATE 37  Hawk moth  *?Eumorpha cissi* Schaufuss [*Sphinx satellitia*]

*Taken 25th July flying at night. Very rare. Called in Savannah Green Hawk moth.*

Plate size 14 × 11 cm. *Insects of Georgia* (Francillon), VII, p. [6], pl. 9

PLATE 36  Squash moth  *?Melitta cucurbitae* (Harris) [*Bombyx*]. Plant:  *Cucurbita pepo* L.

*The caterpillar feeds on the Squash Vine (Cucurbita verrucosa) living in the inside of the large stalks, when it arrives at its full grown it creeps out and goes to the ground, which one did on the 9th July, spinning up in a tough oblong case and bred 6th August. The moth flies in the day and may sometimes be found settled on the leaves of this plant, but it is not common.*

Plate size 23.5 × 30 cm. *Insects of Georgia* (Francillon), XVII, p. [27], pl. 179

of this letter is .16 for a Dollar [6¼ cents], they are mostly small insects and many are minutae ... he must be in possession of 2 or 3000 of them ... .

I shall complete this Autumn my collections of insects and a set of Drawings."[84]

As Abbot grew older, rheumatism gradually began to get the better of him; he became rather corpulent, deaf and his agility lessened. He did not allow this to stop him collecting completely, but the more athletic pursuit of butterflies, which in his younger days had given him so much pleasure, was undertaken by young boys whom he employed for small sums of money. Neverthess, he continued his field trips, albeit rather closer to home, until the year of his death in 1840.[85]

We cannot tell how many specimens Abbot collected in his lifetime. Thousands must have crossed the Atlantic to find a home in European and British collections, and similar numbers must have been in private American collections. Unfortunately, the Abbot specimens, particularly the insects, were usually incorporated into larger collections, and it is now virtually impossible to determine with any certainty which Abbot might have collected himself. Some birds and herbaria are still identifiable and exist in some museum collections.

In his last years, Abbot moved into a small cabin on the land of a friend, William E. McElveen, with his only slave, Betsey, to look after him. In his will he left everything to McElveen, including Betsey:

"Know all men by these presents that I John Abbot of the county and state aforesaid for divers good causes and considerations and the good will and affection which I have and bear to and for my beloved friend Wm. E. McElveen of the same place to all persons to whom these presents shall come Know ye, that I John Abbot do fully give and

grant unto the said Wm McElveen his heirs and assigns my negro woman named Betsey which said negro is in his possession as personal property or effects that I have at my decease to take in his possession as soon as I die without any manner or condition whatever from that time henceforth to be the sole property of the said Wm. E. McElveen his heirs and assigns for ever against the claim of all or any person whatever in witness thereof the said John Abbot hath herunto set his seal this 4th day of June 1839."[86]

There was probably very little to leave, apart from his personal papers and paintings, and it seems that he felt he had done everything possible for his daughter-in-law. John Abbot died in 1840, at the age of eighty-nine, financially poor but rich in reputation for a talent second to none in the illustration of nature.

As soon as Oemler heard of Abbot's death, he approached McElveen, asking to buy his friend's papers at any price. McElveen told him there was nothing to be had: "the children had used all up". If this was so — and there is little to suggest otherwise — it is probable that many valuable paintings, letters and notebooks had been defaced and destroyed. McElveen's comments suggest there were papers of some kind remaining, and that the children had used them for drawing.

Oemler was Abbot's closest friend and confidant, and one must assume that he knew Abbot's circumstances. However, Abbot had written to Swainson in 1835 telling him that he had sent a copy of his book and "all the drawings of insects in my possession". Five years was a long time for Abbot not to put brush to paper.

John Abbot, the man with a "peculiar liking for insects", was buried in an unmarked grave in the McElveen family cemetery, but in 1957 a Georgia Historical Marker was placed in the cemetery, along with a monument bearing a bronze plaque depicting Abbot.

PLATE 38  Wild cotton moth  *Acontia delecta* Wlk. [*Noctuae*]
Plant: Swamp rose mallow  *Hibiscus moscheutos* L. [Wild cotton]
*The caterpillar feeds on wild cotton. It spun up in a case of dirt, on the surface of the ground*
*2nd June and bred 18th June. It is rare.*

Plate size 23 × 30 cm. *Insects of Georgia* (Francillon), XVII, p. [42], pl. 256

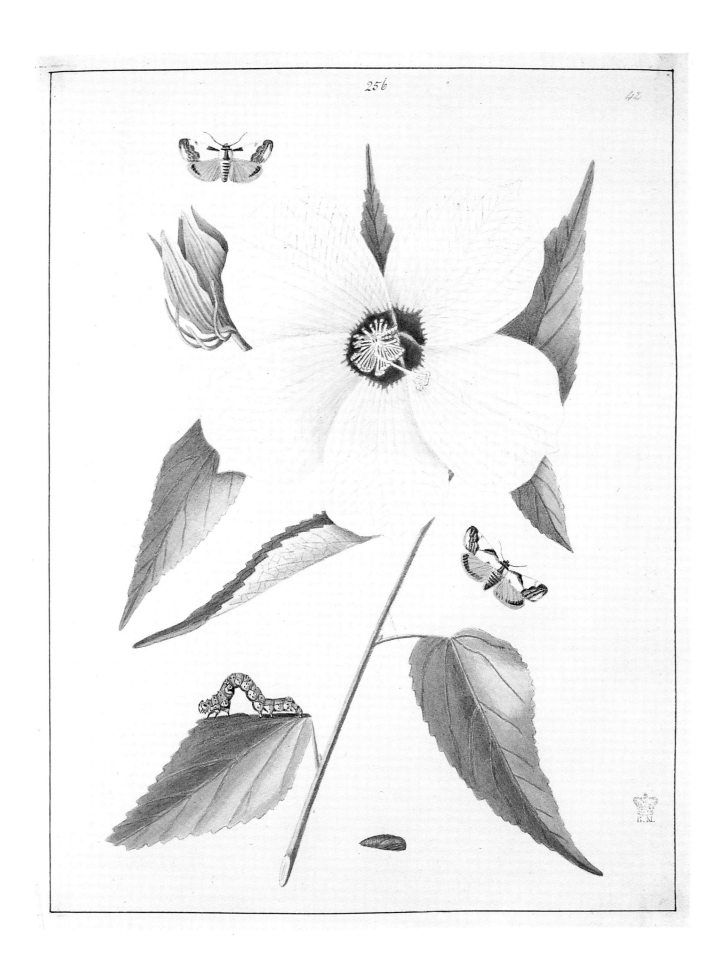

1 Abbot's handwritten 'Notes on my Life', which cover the early years of his life, are held by Harvard University. The 'Notes' were written in old age for his friend Augustus Oemler, and were apparently never completed. They are fully transcribed on pp. 117–24. Uncredited quotations from John Abbot in the text come from the 'Notes'.

2 The change to the Gregorian Calendar in England was made in 1752.

3 Graves (1905); Bennezit (1948); Wilkinson (1984).

4 It is speculated that John Abbot confused Van Dest, who seems not to be known as a "famous flower painter", with the flower painter G.D. Ehret (1708–1770), who often added lepidoptera to his flower paintings. Ehret settled in England in 1736 and lived in London. He married the daughter of Philip Miller, founder of the Chelsea Physic Garden.

5 Wilkinson (1966).

6 Nichols (1817).

7 'Cabinet' was a generic term used to describe collections, and especially collections of natural history specimens. In many grand houses such collections were indeed housed in fine furniture cabinets, but the word is often used to describe rather cruder arrangements.

8 Drewitt (1928); Rougetel (1990).

9 Drury was never in fact president of the Linnean Society, but was certainly elected to the society as a fellow.

10 Reproduced in Noblett (1985); the only known original copy is in the British Library.

11 Anonymous (1816).

12 For example: A.J. Rösel von Rosenhof, *Der Monatlich-herausgegeben Insecten Belustigung*, 4 vols., Nuremberg 1745–61.

Sepp, C., *Beschouwing der Wonderen Gods* ... Amsterdam 1762–1860.

Cramer, P., *De uitlandsche Kapellen* ..., 4 vols., Amsterdam 1775–82.

13 Drury's Ms account book records the sale to Abbot of Vol. 1 of his *Illustrations*, costs of production and listed sales, Entomology Library, The Natural History Museum, London.

14 Letter no. 204, Drury Letter Book, Entomology Library, The Natural History Museum, London.

15 Noblett (1985) mentions some 30,000 volumes being exported across the Atlantic between 1771 and 1774.

16 In addition: *Daily Advertiser* 26 March 1748: "yesterday morning about one o' clock a fire broke out at Mr Elridge's a Peruke-maker in Exchange Alley ... all the Bankers Houses in Lombard Street are safe ... no public office has been burnt. Garraway's, The Jerusalem, and Jonathan's Coffee Houses, the Swan Tavern and the rest of the houses in Change Alley, are destroyed except Baker's and Sam's coffee houses, which are greatly damaged."

17 Jessop (1989); Faulkner (1829).

18 Drury to Linnaeus, Drury Letter Book, Entomology Library, The Natural History Museum, London.

19 Hope (1845), translation of Danish autobiography published 1819.

20 29 August 1787, British Library Add. Ms. 29533, f. 71.

21 Smeathman (1781).

22 Banister (1693).

23 Petiver (1701).

24 Weiss (1926).

25 Sloane Add. Ms 6054, British Museum.

26 Rothstein (1966).

27 Fitton and Gilbert (1994).

28 "Auction" is probably used in the sense of direct sale.

29 Sitwell, Buchanan and Fisher (1953).

30 General Honeywood is listed in the volume as a subscriber.

31 Wilkinson (1984).

32 Drury Letter Book, Entomology Library, The Natural History Museum, London.

33 Goode (1897).

34 *Ibid.*

35 *Ibid.*

36 Parkinson (1978), Abbot letter 1835.

37 Letter from Lord Dartmouth to Lord Dunmore in favour of Mr Abbot, 4 August 1773. Record of commission from the Royal Society, Public Record Office, London, Colonial Office 5, Virginia, vol. 74.

38 Drury Letter Book, letters nos. 269, 270. Entomology Library, The Natural History Museum, London.

39 "ordinary": an inn, or fixed-price meal, *OED* (1989). Such inns were fairly common in Virginia and other parts of the United States, and the Goodalls no doubt supplemented their income in this way. Also Rogers-Price (1983).

40 Goode (1886).

41 Letter no. 315, addressed to Abbot at W. Goodall's near Court House, Hanover County, Virginia, 10 April 1774, Drury Letter Book, Entomology Library, The Natural History Museum, London.

PLATE 39   Rufous border moth [*Noctuae*]. Plant:  *Gentiana* sp.

*The caterpillar feeds on the blue bottle or blue pink crab grasses. etc. It went into the ground 27th Aug. Bred 21st September. It is frequent in the Woods and Plantations flying about the sides of branches of an evening and it frequents plum blossoms in the Spring.*

Plate size 23 × 30 cm. *Insects of Georgia* (Francillon), XVII, p. [67], pl. 163

42 Letter no. 333, 28 November 1774, Drury Letter Book, Entomology Library, The Natural History Museum, London. Also Drury (1801).

43 Letter no. 315, Drury Letter Book, Entomology Library, The Natural History Museum, London.

44 *Ibid.*

45 *Ibid.*

46 Coulter (1960).

47 Hodler and Schretter (1986).

48 Rogers-Price (1983).

49 Hodler and Schretter (1986).

50 Rogers-Price and Griffin (1983); Rogers-Price (1983). The early literature on Abbot indicates that he fought in the Revolution on the American side. The name of Abbot appears in the Surveyor General Records, but as Rogers-Price's extensive research has shown this Abbot signs himself with a cross (X), indicating illiteracy; this could not have been John Abbot the artist.

51 Kirby and Spence, *Introduction to Entomology*, 5th edn., III, 1828, p.148.

52 Rogers-Price (1983).

53 Hodler and Schretter (1986).

54 Rogers-Price (1983).

55 Swainson correspondence, Linnean Society, London.

56 British Library Add. Ms. 295433, ff. 60–83, 87–100.

57 *Ibid.*

58 [Francillon sale catalogue]. An annotated copy is in the Entomology Library of The Natural History Museum, London.

59 C.A. Walckenaer, *Histoire naturelle des Insectes Aptères*, 1837–47.

60 Rogers-Price (1983).

61 Stroud (1992).

62 Smith and Abbot (1797), introduction.

63 Smith mentions the authors of several magnificent entomological works with coloured illustrations. Although all were well respected works at the time, Smith points out that they lacked the first-hand information supplied by Abbot on food and habitat, and the detailed information on the metamorphosis of the butterflies depicted:

C.A. Clerck, *Icones insectorum rariorum nominibus eorum trivialibus*, 3 parts, 1739.

P. Cramer, *De vitlandsche kapellen (Papillons exotiques des trois parties du monde, l'Asie, l'Afrique et l'Amerique*, 4 vols., 1775–82.

G.A. Olivier, *Entmologie, ou histoire naturelle des insectes: Coléoptères*, 6 vols. and atlas.

64 J.E. Smith Mss., Linnean Society, London.

65 John Abbot had painted insects and shells for George Humphrey before he left London.

66 Swainson correspondence, Linnean Society, London.

67 *Ibid.*

68 Hunter (1983).

69 *Ibid.*

70 Cantwell (1961).

71 Dr Benjamin Barton, author of *Fragments of Natural History of Pennsylvania*.

72 Hunter (1983), letter 143; this also shows that Abbot had copies of Smith and Abbot.

73 Letter to Ord.

74 Heinrich Escher-Zollikofer.

75 Swainson correspondence, Linnean Society, London.

76 Abbot to Swainson, Savannah, Georgia, 20 December 1816:

"I shall expect be able to complete about 100 [drawings] by the time I shall have your collection of insects ready for you. I have always not had less than 7/6 sterling a piece for such drawings, but I am willing to take 6s a piece for these ... The spiders of Georgia being numerous and many remarkable for size and beauty I have an intention of Drawing a set of 5 on a size drawings in the manner of Albin if you or any friend should be desirous to purchase them I have no doubt we shall agree on a price."

Swainson to Abbot, 25 October 1817, Bahia, Brazil:

"I know not whether I mentioned to you that I was specially anxious you should send me all the species of Papilio and sphinx you can meet with, among the former I am most desirous of the different species of skippers as they are termed in England and which come under the division of Hesperia ... bicolor of Linnaeus of the interesting family I have found in Brazil more than 100 species.
    Secondly – with respect to drawings I am perfectly willing to take a

PLATE 40 Royal walnut moth   *Cithronia regalis* (Fabricius) [The Emperial (*sic*) or Great Royal Persimmon Moth, *Bombyx Regia*]
Plant: Persimmon, or American date plum   *Diospyros virginiana* (L.)

*The caterpillar feeds on Persimmon, Summach, Hickory and Walnut. It went into the ground 15th August, the moth was Bred 28th April and some were not bred until May and June. This caterpillar when disturbed shakes its head about very nimbly and makes a very formidable appearance, and is vulgarly dreaded as much as a rattlesnake. It is called by some the Hickory Horn Devil. This species is very thinly scattered all over the continent as very seldom more than one at a time are to be met with on a Tree and it is very rarely met with in the Moth State.*

Plate size 23 × 30 cm. *Insects of Georgia* (Francillon), XVI, p. [86], pl. 22

series of Drawings of all the species of Papilio and Sphinx which are not figured in Smith's work ... provided you can accompany them with drawings of their metamorphosis."

Abbot to Swainson, 1 May 1819, Savannah:

"I have sent you a large box of insects containing 900. The loss of Mrs Abbot and my own sickness last Autmn has occasioned the delay ... I have likewise sent you under cork at the bottom of the box (being a false bottom) 104 Q[uarto] drawings ... making a second volume to Smith.

"The loss of Mrs Abbot has caused me to leave of the housekeeping, and as I am now unsettled – should be glad to go to some other part to collect. ... if it would afford the opportunity to collect shells for Mr Swainson your father it would still be better."

Abbot to Swainson, 7 June 1819, Savannah:

"I will first propose in regard of the drawing that I will draw over again for you, these that you want that are not in Smith's work of the size you want but which you most particulariy mention in your next at 5s sterling each ... meet with a new flower or plant much pleases me My friend Mr Oemler of Savannah says he will take the plants off my hands ... I had thoughts of taking a trip to the back state of Tenneessee to collect insects and birds, but I think when Florida is taken possession of and settled by the United States, it will afford ample field for collecting if life and health permits."

Abbot was still anxious not to get mixed up in any revolutionary actions and was probably taking the right decisions. Abbot to Swainson, 16 June 1819:

"My correspondent a Mr. Escher a gentleman from Switzerland lately a Merchant of New York but now resides in his native country Switzerland. It will be best therefore to ship the insects to him and not to me, according to his directions which I shall add at the last part of this letter ... 2000 Insects half Lepidoptera, the others Coleoptera Hymenoptera and Diptera ... these in a large box preserved from the damp, to be sent to Mr Henry Escher ... writing them, a few lines to request their utmost care for the box and directing them to forward it by the best possible route per waggon to Mr Henry Escher-Zollikofer in Switzerland after having carefully put up in straw and tow cloth and marked outside with blacking which is the upper side."

The paintings for another volume of Smith would have been for a third volume – Abbot's own volume may have been bound as one. A third volume was never published; the publishers did not believe the work had sold well enough and refused to enter into publication of a third volume.

77  Swainson correspondence, Archives of the Linnean Society, London.

78  Ewan (1963).

79  Baldwin to Mühlenberg, 4 November, 1811, Lancaster. Darlington (1843), p. 52.

80  Largen and Rogers-Price1 (1985); Simpson (1993).

81  Bassett (1938); Rogers-Price (1983).

82  Parkinson (1978).

83  Dow (1914).

84  *Ibid.*

85  *Ibid.*

86  Bassett (1938).

PLATE 41 [Plum Lackey Moth, *Bombyx Castrensis*]
Plant: *Prunus insititia* L. [Common Bullace Plum Tree]

*The caterpillar feeds on Plum, Apple and Cherry laurel. These caterpillars in broods together making a Web in common for their security, they spun up 18th April, Bred 24th May. The moth is not common but the caterpillars are very frequent. I have seen such numbers in a Apple Orchard in Virginia as nearly to eat all the leaves. but they are not so common in these parts.*

Plate size 23 × 30 cm. *Insects of Georgia* (Francillon), XVI, p. [114], pl. 92

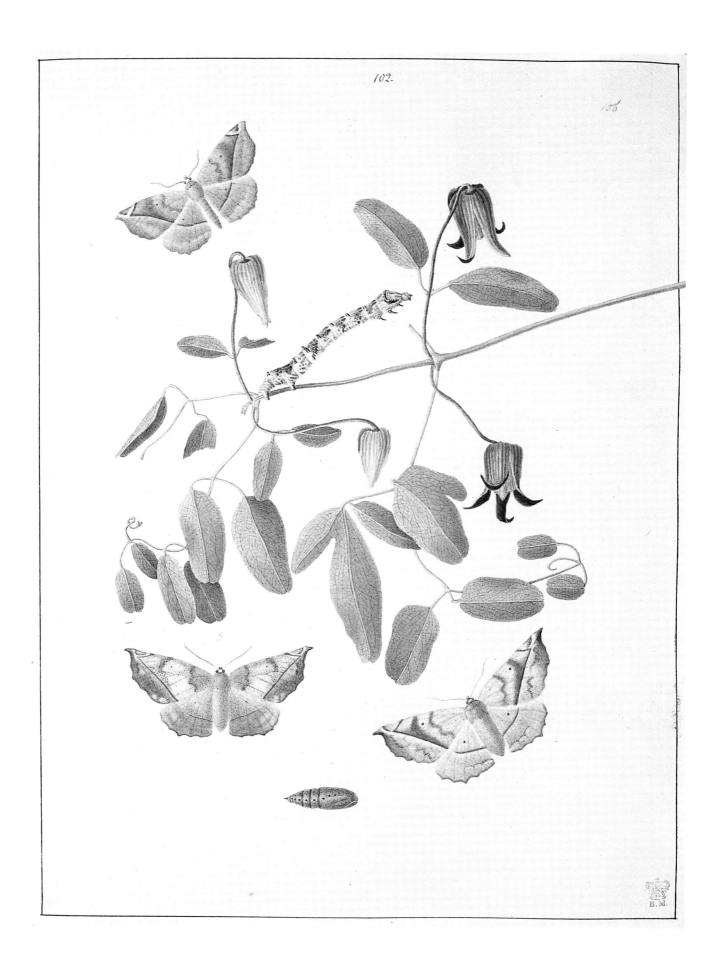

# The Practicalities

## "Masterpieces of Entomological Portraiture"

Before leaving London, Abbot had produced a considerable portfolio of watercolours, including thirteen painted from Drury's specimens. These so called London drawings are deposited in the United States.[1] One set, now in the Houghton Library, Harvard University, seems to have been disposed of just before Abbot left for Virginia, but there are no records to show what happened to it between then and 1912, almost a hundred and forty years later, when it was sold by the London dealers Bernard Quaritch and acquired later by the Boston Natural History Society from the Harvard University's Museum of Comparative Zoology. Later still, the collection was returned to Harvard, where it remains. A second set of watercolours is in the library of the Carnegie Museum in Pittsburgh. This second set was owned by the Russian entomologist Andrei Avinoff (1884–1949) and taken by him to America when he was forced to flee from Russia in 1917.[2] All his other possessions, including an unrivalled entomological collection and library (which was later burned), had to be left behind. In his one suitcase, he allowed himself this one treasure – a single volume of Abbot watercolours, which he described as "masterpieces of entomological portraiture". Avinoff was to become Director of the Carnegie Museum and eventually bequeathed his Abbot paintings to the museum. An enthusiastic admirer of Abbot's paintings, he describes how, "Every hook or minutest spine is recorded with oustanding precision .... The lustre of elytra and transparency of wings is never lost by an excess of detail."

In his 'Notes', Abbot records the loss of two collections (containing both entomological specimens and paintings), despatched to England from Virginia, but losses of translatlantic sailing ships were high, and it seems a strong possibility that others were lost over the years.

After Abbot moved to Georgia, he spent the best part of sixty-five years providing specimens and watercolours for his customers, with only one short break of less than twelve months in 1812. By 1813, requests for watercolours of both birds and insects sent him back to work, and it is the paintings that survive in large numbers. One estimate is for about 5000 extant paintings, but the actual number is not known; Abbot paintings still come on to

PLATE 42 Looper moth *Eutrapela clemataria* (Smith) [Great hook tip Looper Moth, *Geometrae clemataria*] Plant: *Clematis reticulatus* Walt. [Rose colour'd Virgin's Bower, *Clematis Rosea Nova* sp. *Reticulata* Walt. Flor. Carol. 186.]

*The caterpillar was taken on the Maiden's Bower, it also eats Alder and Sassafrass etc. and is fond of the tender leaves of Holly. It spun up in the leave 18th April. Bred 24th May, another that spun up on 23rd June Bred 8th August. Fig. 5 is a variety of the Female. It chiefly frequents swamps and Hammocks and the Moth may be found at night on Plum Blossom but is not common.*

Similar to plate 101 in Smith and Abbot 1797. The plant position differs, and the male and female undersides are shown.

Plate size 23 × 30.5 cm. *Insects of Georgia* (Francillon), XVII, p. [106], pl. 102

the market. In spite of numerous enquiries, the only known holding in continental Europe is that of the Bibliothèque Centrale du Muséum National d'Histoire Naturelle in Paris. However, given the number of clients Abbot is known to have had on the Continent, it is very possible that other paintings exist, unidentified. There are, by contrast, numerous collections in libraries and museums in the United States, and many individual paintings in private hands. The largest single deposit of Abbot paintings is that held in The Natural History Museum in London. These include the insect and spider paintings that Francillon bought for his own collection, together with two volumes of insect paintings and one volume of bird paintings from the Rothschild bequest.

By 1790, Abbot had completed a first large set of watercolours of insects for Francillon in London, and more followed, for Francillon to sell on to naturalists in England and Europe. Francillon himself became such an admirer of Abbot's watercolours that he bought many for himself, owning well over 3000 – of both birds and particularly insects – by the time of his death in 1816. Francillon divided the paintings of insects and other invertebrates into seventeen volumes, uniformly bound in red full leather and containing Abbot's notes. In some cases he copied Abbot's notes and added some of his own, particularly in volume 14 containing the spider paintings. Abbot's own numbers remained on the paintings, although Francillon numbered the pages in the bound volumes himself. Customers might be invited to view Francillon's collection of paintings and order by Abbot's number or Francillon's page number. The resulting painting often varied slightly in pose or background. Some of the paintings have Linnean names which

Francillon probably added, judging by a letter to Phillips in Manchester (see p. 104), in which he says he has checked as many of Abbot's names as possible and has estimated that not "one tenth part of them [the species] is described".[3] On Francillon's death, these seventeen volumes were bought 'for the Nation' by the British Museum with special funds, at a cost of £300, and formed part of their natural history collections. They were later transferred to the new (1881) British Museum (Natural History) in South Kensington (subsequently renamed The Natural History Museum).

The set of bird paintings was acquired by Lionel Walter Rothschild (1868–1937) in 1889 for his own library, then part of his museum at Tring in Hertfordshire, but its earlier provenance is not known. The two insect volumes were acquired by Rothschild at a later date, and carry the bookplate of Sir Robert Johnson Eden, Bart. Upon Rothschild's death in 1937, his collections and library were bequeathed to the nation and administered by what is now The Natural History Museum.

In 1883, Dr Gunther, Keeper of the Department of Zoology in South Kensington, requested the transfer of the seventeen Francillon volumes of Abbot paintings from the Department of Manuscripts in the British Museum to the new Natural History museum.[4] He wanted them for the use of the scientific staff, and it would seem that he played down the importance of the manuscript notes in order to pry the paintings out of the hands of the Trustees of the British Museum. The application was successful, and in spite of an offer to refund the purchase price to the Trustees, no money ever changed hands.

Gunther, however keen to acquire the Francillon

PLATE 43 Tulip-tree moth *Epimecis hortaria* F. [Carpet or Tulip-Tree beauty, *Geometra Liriodedraria*]
Plant: Yellow poplar *Liriodedron tulipifera* (Linn.) [Common Tulip Tree]

*The caterpillar feeds on the Tulip Tree (called in Georgia), Poplar and Sassafrass; it spun up on 11th July. was bred the 1st August. It frequents swamps and the Oak Woods. The Moth may sometimes be found settled on the bodies of large trees. In the night it frequents Plum and other blossoms. It is not very common.*

Plate 102 in Smith and Abbot 1797. The lower moth is in a different position and the flower position is not the same.

Plate size 23.3 × 30 cm. *Insects of Georgia* (Francillon), XVII, p. [99], pl. 59

volumes, was not complimentary about the painting, comparing it, to Abbot's disadvantage, with that of August Johann Roesel (1705–1759), the German author, entomologist and expert painter of miniatures. J.E. Smith, on the other hand, who had collaborated with Abbot in his *Natural History of the rarer Lepidopterous Insects of Georgia*, had been strong in his admiration for Abbot's work – particularly the paintings showing the metamorphosis of butterflies and moths. Adrian Hardy Haworth (1767–1833),[5] an eminent English lepidopterist and botanist and close friend of Smith, was another early admirer of Abbot's work. In 1807, he reviewed the rise of interest in entomology in Great Britain in the *Transactions of the Entomological Society of London*, and described the Smith and Abbot work as "truly a Flora et Entomologia" – of value both to the botanist and to the entomologist.

Another bequest to the British Museum (Natural History) was that of the naturalist Thomas de Grey, Lord Walsingham (1843–1919), who later became a Trustee of the museum. Grey bequeathed all his collections and his library, and among the manuscripts was a set of paintings labelled "148 [248] paintings of moths of Georgia by John Abbot". The earlier provenance of this collection is not known. Although labelled in this way, the paintings are not of the usual Abbot quality. The paintings of moths, each on a separate sheet, have no embellishments and no notes; the colouring is poor and it is doubtful whether they are by Abbot.

As Abbot's skills progressed, so his style changed. Some of the early paintings depicting butterflies show the specimens with their wings open and flat, rather like cabinet specimens; later, he tended towards a more naturalistic pose, showing the wings closed in a resting position, illustrating the upper and under sides of the wings separately. He was acutely aware of the requirements of his customers. Writing to Smith about *The Natural History of the rarer Lepidopterous Insects of Georgia*, he says:

"The Butterflies I have figured both upper and underside, as the underside of most is remarkably different, as of many is the only material [character to distinguish the species] as in the meadow brown, ringlets, blues and hair streaks etc.

But as the [undersides of the] moths [have] uniform sameness, generally of pale colours, something resembling the upper, [and which are rarely exhibited] in cabinets I think a slight description sufficient. Neither have I drawn any in their sitting posture [or with their wings unexpanded] as I think that immaterial, as they commonly hide their most beautiful colours when at rest, neither are they admitted in that posture into the Cabinets of the Curious."[6]

Never an enthusiastic botanist or plant painter, his first attempts to paint plants were not exceptional; nevertheless, after some coaching by Oemler, this also improved. He wrote to Swainson, 7 June 1819, "I am no Botanist, but only an admirer of natures beauties, to meet with a new flower or plant much pleases me ... ."[7] He was anxious to be just as accurate with the plants as with the insects, considering them an essential part of his paintings.

Many of the watercolours that Abbot sent to Francillon included the food plants of his subjects, but

Plate 44   Streaked American tiger moth   *Grammia argue* (Drury) [*Bombyx Dione*]
Plant: Sunflower  *Helianthus* sp.

*The caterpillar feeds on the wild Marygold, Corn Peas and, many other plants. It was hatched from the Egg 23rd July. Spun up 28th August. Bred 9th Septr. Another spun up on 28th May, Bred 9th June, But it is not very common.*
Perhaps one of Abbot's cruder early illustrations. Both the plant and the insect have a particularly flat appearance: he had not yet come to terms with botanical illustration.

Plate size 23 × 30 cm. *Insects of Georgia* (Francillon), XVI, p. [119], pl. 118

earlier paintings done in London had no such embellishments and depicted the insects in tabular form – the common style of illustrated books of the time.

From the few records of Abbot's comments on his work, it is clear that he had studied the illustrative work of other artists and had learned to mix and grind his own pigments. He writes to Smith:[8]

"... in some of my first drawings the greens turned blackish, owing to my use of Sap Green, I now quite discarded it to use a mixture of Green [Bouge] and Indigo, but again find that this fades a little. Albin in his Hist. of Insects says he has not painted them of too bright colours, but like myself he falls much short of the originals for want of sufficient bright colours. Brooks in his system[9] says a bad drawing conveys as good an idea as a good one; he stands in need of such as excuse for his bad copies of Mouffet's insects etc. However, I think Albin had merit considering the time [1720] he published his work, but Brook's Testeem [is] but as a bookseller's latch-penny."[10]

Albin had produced a formula for vermillion, but it is questionable whether Abbot followed his advice to wash and dry the pigment in four waters and then grind it in boy's urine three times before adding gum to it and grinding in brandywine![11]

Walton (1921)[12] praises Abbot for his attainments and inordinate skill, commenting on his skilful use of pigments: "The choice and application of the pigments evinces the work of a consummate expert, as the colours today are as brilliant as though they had been applied yesterday and there appears no trace of the oxidation which mars many of the older coloured illustrations of insects where the pigments have been chosen without regard to their chemical affinity and possible reaction upon each other."

Those pigments are still bright and clear, with virtually no fading. Abbot always used pure watercolours for his work, experimenting with the pigments available to him to obtain the colours he wanted, and relying on colour to indicate textures, rather than additions to the medium. Only occasionally did he use gum arabic, with which many artists enhanced their paintings. He was a master of manipulating colours to indicate transparency of wings and iridescence of wings and elytra.

Abbot took with him to America large quantities of good quality, heavy duty Watman paper, having found that this took watercolour well. His paintings, with one exception, are all graphite on paper, and coloured. The second portrait that is believed to be of John Abbot, supposedly a self-portrait and held by Emory University in Atlanta, appears to be a charcoal sketch and is uncoloured (fig. 18).[13]

Abbot's watercolours and biological observations rank high among the contributors from North America in the late eighteenth and nineteenth century. The little of Abbot's work that was published does poor justice to the originals. Abbot had no control over the engraving or the final production of the plates, and it is unfortu-

Plate 45  Robin moth  *Hyalophora cecropia* (Linn.) [Great Brown Emperor Moth, *Bombyx cecropia*]
Plant:  *Prunus* sp. [Wild American Plum, *Prunus Pensylvanica* Linn.]

*The caterpillar feeds on the Wild Plum (figured) Apple Redroot etc. It spun up 3rd September in a web fastened to the branch of a Tree. The chrysalis is enclosed in an Inner Web resembling that of a silk worm. The moth was bred 16th March. I have been informed that the inner web, mixed and carded with cotton has been made into a pair of stockings for curiosity but are too thinly scattered and rare and are too tender to raise and Breed them from the Egg, same as the silk worms. Therefore, they cannot be rendered useful in any large quantity.*

Very similar to plate 45 in Smith and Abbot 1797. This was the first published illustration showing the entire life cycle of this moth.

Plate size 23.3 × 30 cm. *Insects of Georgia* (Francillon), VI, p. [88], pl. 24

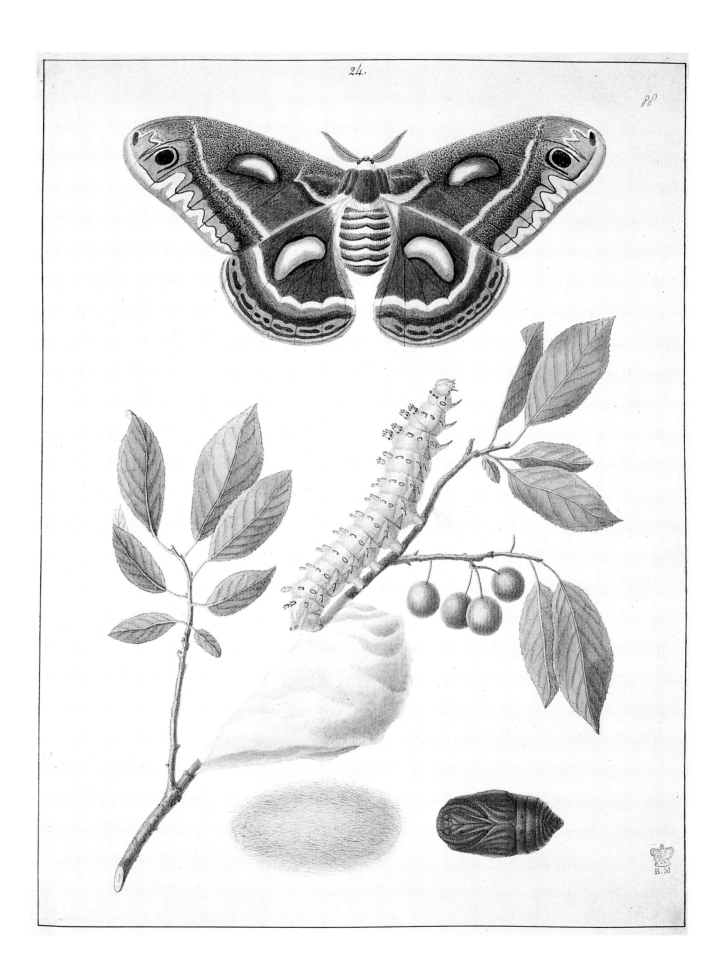

26 Portrait of John Le Conte (1748–1860)

27 Identification table from Vol. 14 (Spiders) of Abbot's watercolours in The Natural History Museum, London

nate that his skill in conveying subtlety of colours and surface textures could not be reproduced accurately by the techniques of the time. One might speculate how spectacular the plates would have been, had he learned to do his own engraving as George Edwards had done,[14] and if he had been able to supervise the colouring artists.

Plates were always hand-coloured and small armies of itinerant artists were employed to copy the original pattern plates. One set, sometimes more, of engraved plates would be coloured by the artist, and these would be given to the colourists to copy. Variations in colour often resulted, and some of the coloured plates were not beautiful; they were nevertheless useful aids to the interested naturalist.

For many years Abbot supplied his neighbour in Georgia, Major John Eatton Le Conte (1748–1860) (fig. 26), with watercolours and specimens. T.W. Harris was under the impression that Le Conte was Abbot's sole financial supporter, but Oemler wrote to him in 1834 rather tersely, to contradict this: "… as far as [Abbot] to be supported by Major Le Conte that is not so, except for the petty allowance of six and a quarter cents per drawing of an insect",[15] and Abbot himself wrote to Harris: "… my charge to Mr Le Conte for my drawings and for whom I continue to draw every year is 1.6 for a dollar … he must be in possession of 2-3000 of them."[16]

Le Conte was a man of means; he had inherited wealth and was the owner of a large plantation. He had an enthusiasm for natural history and for lepidoptera in particular, and was eager to publish a work on the lepidoptera of America, with Abbot's paintings and specimens forming the basis of the work. Abbot was

PLATE 46 Pea moth  *Platynota rostrana* (Walker). Plant: *Lilium* sp.

*Taken on the flower figured but is frequent on the Pea vines. Spun to the side of the box 15th of August. Bred the 23rd is not very common.*

Plate size 31.5 × 22.5 cm. *Insects of Georgia* (Rothschild bequest), I, pl. 61

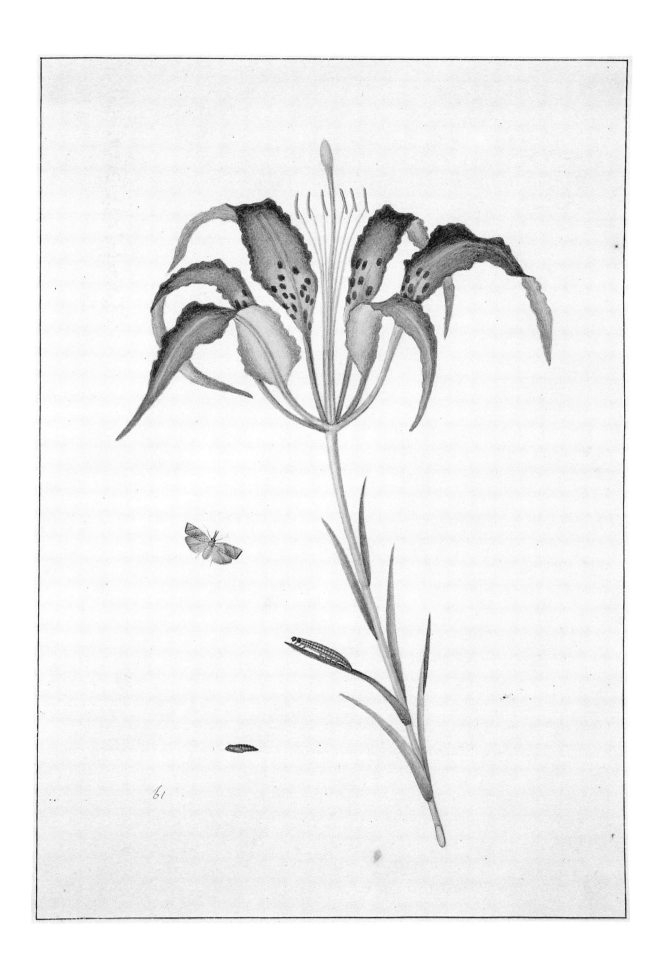

61

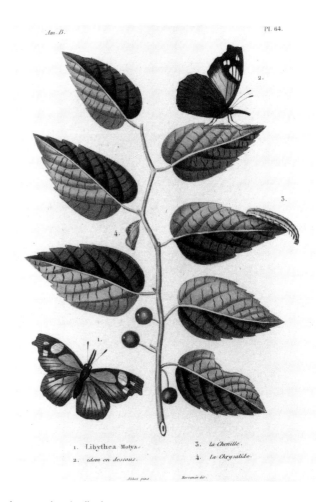

28, 29 Plates from Le Conte and Boisduval, *Histoire générale et Iconographie des Lépidoptères et des Chenilles de L'Amérique septentrionale* (1829–34)

instructed to draw only the adults, larvae and pupae. There were to be no plants and the male and female were only to be depicted if they obviously differed (figs. 28, 29). Abbot did not always adhere to these instructions.

In 1825, Le Conte travelled to Paris to show his collection to the renowned French entomologist J.A. Boisduval (1801–1879), and it was eventually agreed that the two naturalists would publish the work, *Histoire générale et Iconographie des Lépidoptères et des Chenilles de l'Amérique septentrionale*, between them. Abbot's paintings were used for

nearly all the plates, but he had no control over their production and saw neither engravings nor proofs before publication. The early plates, engraved by Duméril, were not a success and several subscribers complained to the publishers. Boisduval was forced to publish an announcement (*Avis*) with his tenth delivery:

"Certain of our subscribers have complained that, although our figures are accurately coloured, they are not well drawn (engraved); most of the bodies are defective,

PLATE 47 *Marathyssa* sp. [Shumach Moth]. Plant: *Rhus copallina*

*Feeds on the Schumach [sic]. Went into the ground the 23rd May. Spun in a case covered in dirt.*
*Bred the 26th June. It is not very common.*

Plate size 28.5 × 23.5 cm. *Insects of Georgia* (Rothschild bequest), II, pl. 79

79

with the wings and legs badly attached and the veins faulty ... subscribers may be assured that from Delivery 10 our figures will not longer show these faults." [translation]

After Borromée (*fl.* 1828–31) was brought in to do the rest of the engravings, there was a distinct improvement. Cowan (1869) suggests that Duméril had done his best with "sometimes imperfect originals", but there was no other criticism of Abbot's originals.[17] Although Abbot got some small financial recompense for his paintings, it is doubtful whether he received a fee after publication; he certainly received scant recognition for his contribution to the work.

Abbot's English naturalist friend William Swainson (see p. 68) was the recipient of several hundred Abbot watercolours, including 103 which he bought in 1818. These had been intended for an additional volume to Smith's *The Natural History of the rarer Lepidopterous Insects of Georgia.*[18] Unfortunately, the publisher, James Edwards, had lost money on the original venture, and when Francillon, as early as 1803, had tried to get Edwards to produce another volume, offering him his own drawings "without any fee or reward", Edwards had declined. Abbot of course had received nothing for the original publication. Edwards died in 1816, but watermarks in the paper of some copies show that some of the plates were reissued between 1817 and 1827. Perhaps the company had sought to recoup its losses by reprinting. Eventually the copperplates were acquired by the London publisher and engraver R. Martin, but no second edition was ever printed.

In 1835, Abbot wrote to Swainson telling him that he had "sent 670 plates, about 650 drawings of single insects on small papers being all the drawings of insects in my possession", and that "I have put my book and other drawings at the bottom of the box."[19] This could per-haps explain why there was no residue of paintings left when Abbot died.

Swainson was himself an excellent artist, and, in 1820, began publishing *Zoological Illustrations*; Abbot of course knew of Swainson's ability as a collector but there is no evidence that he knew of his friend's artistic talent.

Swainson's wife died about the time of Abbot's death, leaving him with five children, and the drawings in his possession were probably taken to New Zealand when he emigrated there with his family in 1841. The water-colours were eventually acquired by the Turnbull Library in Wellington, New Zealand, in 1927. In 1983, the Turnbull Library initiated a project to publish facsimile copies of the plates, but only six have appeared, and it seems unlikely that the project will continue. "My book" that Swainson was sent was presumably the *Lepidoptera of Georgia*, but Parkinson (1978) states that no copy of this work exists in New Zealand or Australia, so Swainson pre-sumably sold it before leaving England. He was desper-ately in need of funds, and the sale of this and other paintings would have given him a good financial start.

Swainson was among the first to write a biographical sketch of Abbot, but some of the facts in his *Cabinet Cyclopaedia* (1840) are questionable:

"These drawings are so beautiful, chaste and wonder-fully correct, that they are coverted by everyone. So many in fact applied for them, both in Europe and America, that he found it expedient to employ one or two assis-tants, whose copies he retouched ... and thus finished, they generally pass as his own."

Abbot's meticulous work over the years mark him as a man of integrity; this very trait makes it unlikely that he would have passed off something not entirely of his own to his customers without telling them.

PLATE 48 [Little Red Underwing]. Plant: *Arisaema* sp.

*Feeds on the plant figured, and others. Spun the 11th September. Bred the 4th April.*
*The moth is frequent in the woods and fields.*

Plate size 33.5 x 24 cm. *Insects of Georgia* (Rothschild bequest), II, pl. 102

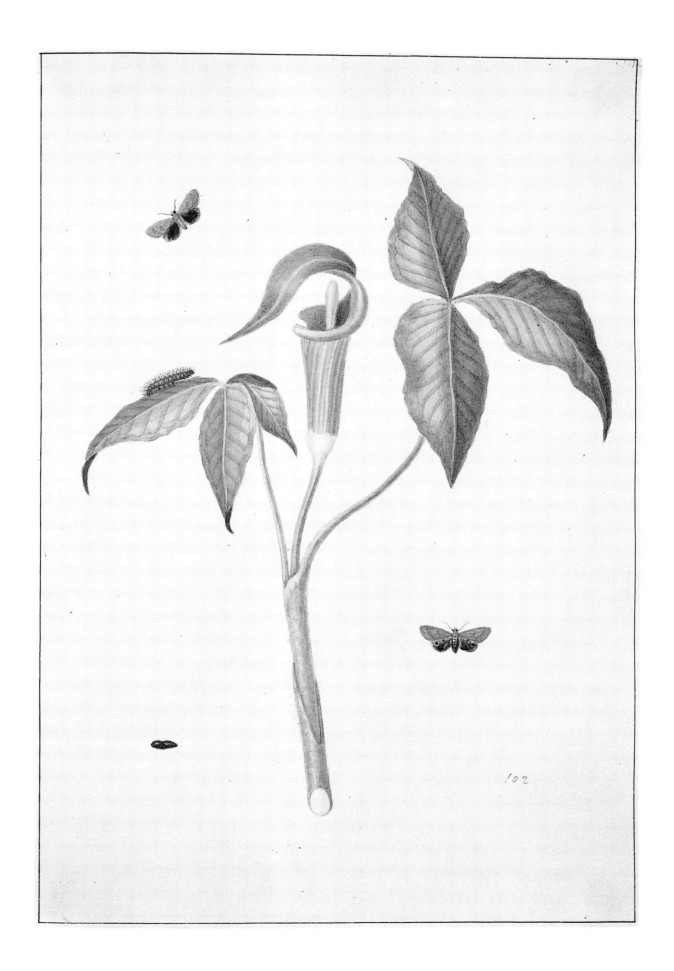

102

Abbot certainly produced duplicates and copies of some of his plates. As we have seen, the paintings in Francillon's bound volumes were numbered so that patrons could order from them. He kept a pattern book of paintings and copies of his notes on his subjects. Writing to Stephen Elliot (see p. 66), he says: "... if you take any more watercolours please send me the numbers of each in the corner, so that I may not mistake in sending what you already have got, and that I may send the notes of each, to illustrate the history of each insect."

Abbot's work was known and appreciated in Europe, but many private individuals in his adopted country also bought from him, and recognition came from his local community. The Savannah Library Society (of which Oemler had been a founder member and librarian) arranged to buy a set of watercolours depicting insect metamorphosis in association with food plants, and, in 1813, bought a further set of 80 watercolours for the library.[20] The American botanist William Baldwin (see p. 74) frequently visited Abbot and knew his work well. In 1811, he wrote to Dr Mühlenberg enthusing about the paintings acquired for the library.[21]

In 1805, the Bavarian lepidopterist Jacob Hübner (1761–1826) began publishing his *Sammlung exotischer Schmetterlinge*, a work in which he described and illustrated some of the Georgian lepidopterous fauna, probably based on specimens and paintings obtained from Francillon. In 1949, The Natural History Museum bought, with the help of Friends of National Libraries, the Baron von Rosen collection – original drawings and manuscripts by Hübner and other contemporary authors, and some small watercolours of lepidoptera by Abbot.

Abbot was also an enthusiastic collector of spiders, and fulfilled many orders for watercolour drawings. He sent Francillon a set of 582 watercolours, which Francillon bound as Vol. 14 of his complete set. Only the first of the paintings is signed by Abbot, and dated 1800. There is, however, an extensive introduction by Abbot:

"The collecting and making of these drawings has been the work for many years observations but more particularly has engaged my attention for these last seven years. Spiders are very numerous in this country and many of a size far superior to that in England. They are also much larger than any I observed in Virginia, and the other Northern States; some of them are very curious shapes of great beauty, are local and very rare; others are common and dispersed all over the country."

Abbot also supplied a table as an aid to identification (fig. 27) – a new venture:

"I have not attempted in the drawings to arrange or divide the spiders in any regular manner, but they may be divided and subdivided like other animals ... However, I have made the following divisions as a hint to the most skiful in natural history."

Francillon carefully examined and collated the collections received from Abbot, and his annotations can be clearly seen in this volume of drawings. He indicates in careful detail the males and females of the species even though they are frequently protrayed on different plates:

"(1st drawing) ... this is the male at No. 281 (57th Drawing)
(8th drawing) ... 417 is I believe the female to No. 197 (40th drawing)"

Among the introductory notes he introduces a reference to a species depicted in a previous volume:

"See the genus Sphex No 50 and 67 and Vespa 53 in the 12th Volume."

PLATE 49  Hibiscus looper [*Geometridae*]. Plant: *Hibiscus* sp.

*Taken on the Hibiscus specimens. I have also met with it on Hickory. Went into ground on the 29th June. Bred the 13th July. Is not common.*

Plate size 33.5 × 24 cm. *Insects of Georgia* (Rothschild bequest), II, pl. 108

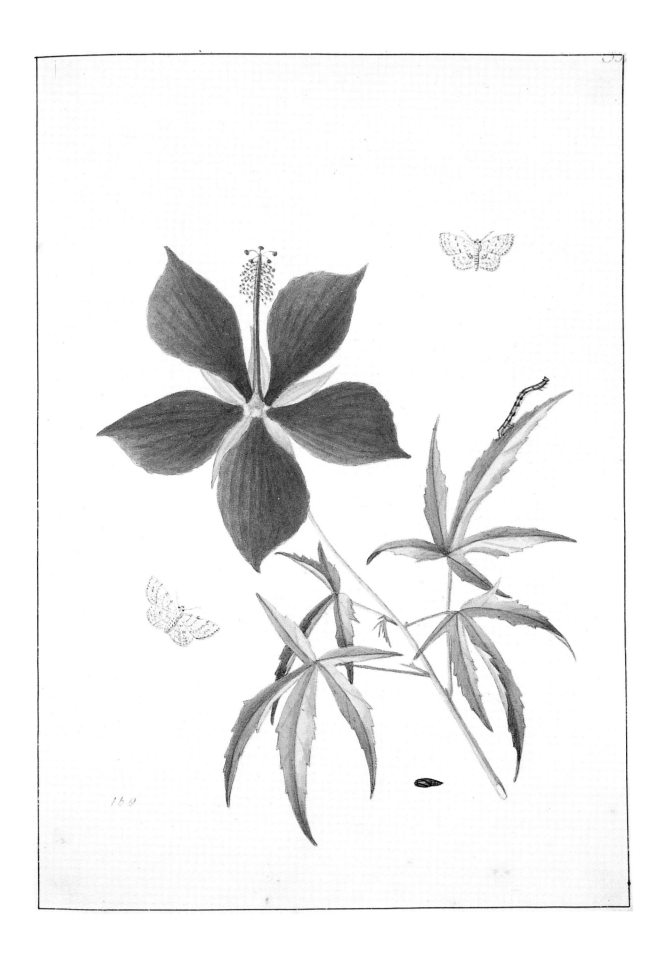

168

Chamberlain and Ivie (1944) state that Charles Athanase Walckenaer (1771–1852) bought these watercolours from Abbot in 1821, and assume they were bought by the British Museum from the Walckenaer estate on his death. Certainly, Walckenaer's *Histoire naturelle des Insectes Aptères* (1837–47) was based on the illustrations in this volume, but it seems more likely that the paintings had been loaned to him by Francillon; it was not uncommon for Francillon to do this. Walckenaer's book includes many of Francillon's additional notes and, as usual, copies of Abbot's own notes. There is no evidence in the minutes of the Trustees of the British Museum that this volume was separately purchased; it is bound uniformly with the red leather of the previous volumes and, like the others, carries Francillon's personal bookplate. Walckenaer did own another set of Abbot paintings of spiders, which he had bought from a friend and entomologist, Mackay, and which he also used. This set of 'Abbot's Georgian Spiders' is in the Bibliothèque Centrale du Muséum National d'Histoire Naturelle in Paris.[22]

Abbot had established a routine for collecting, breeding, drawing and preserving insects; he adopted a similar routine for his birds. He had recognized the importance of painting his insects alive, or while still fresh, before the colours faded, and applied the same principles to the birds. The birds also had to be skinned, stuffed and preserved for customers who had requested specimens rather than paintings. He had not painted birds before leaving for America, so probably needed to hone his skills before sending his first collection of a hundred bird paintings to Francillon in 1792. Francillon immediately showed these watercolours to his friend John Latham (see p. 62) who, impressed, studied them carefully and made several annotations to the plates. Francillon writes: "... if he collected drawings he would certainly have purchased them."[23] Latham was a surgeon and one of the co-founders of the Linnean Society. He

had been elected a Fellow of the Royal Society in 1775, and after acquiring a huge fortune from his practice, retired from medicine in 1796 to pursue his all-absorbing interest in ornithology. He had already published *A General Synopsis of Birds* (1781–85) and *Index ornithologicus* (1790), and was in the midst of preparing an additional volume of the *General Synopsis* when Francillon showed him Abbot's watercolours.

Later, Latham did buy both skins and paintings direct from Abbot, with Abbot's usual biological notes attached. Latham acknowledges the information he received from Abbot in the supplement to his *General Synopsis*. Six volumes of Latham's original drawings are in The Natural History Museum library, and among them are six bird portraits and six anatomical plates, including the trachea of the hooded merganser (*Lopholytes cucollatus* Linn.), inscribed *J. Abbot. delin.*, of about 1828. It was unusual for Abbot to do anatomical drawings, but, as ever, he did what his patrons requested.

Francillon was industrious in seeking buyers for Abbot's specimens and watercolours, and eventually sold this initial collection of bird portraits to Chethams Library in Manchester. John Leigh Phillips (1761–1814), a wealthy Manchester merchant who had developed a strong interest in natural history and who helped many impoverished naturalists, was instrumental in helping Francillon to place his collection with the Gentlemen (Governors) of the library.[24] He and Francillon corresponded regularly, and Francillon presumably assumed that he had here a ready market for additional Abbot collections; but there were problems. The Governors agreed to take further paintings and Abbot agreed to start painting immediately, but inevitably it was a long time before the next batch was sent. In the meantime, a new librarian had been appointed, who was less than happy with the paintings when they finally arrived in 1805. Much to Francillon's dismay, the order was cancelled.

PLATE 50 [Belted Cimex]. Upper: *Venesa* sp. (Coreidae). Lower: *Hammatocerus* sp. Reduviidae

*Frequents the James-town weed (Datura stramonium). Shed its skin the 18th July.*

*This cimex is common in all parts of the Country.*

Plate size 29 × 23 cm. *Insects of Georgia* (Rothschild bequest), I, pl. 3

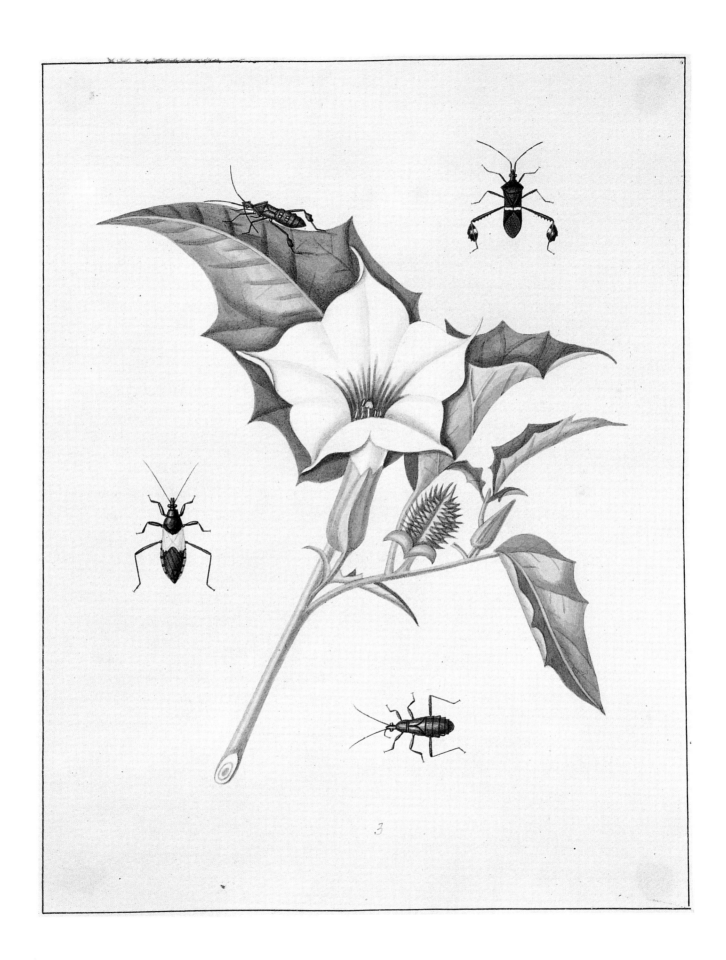

3

However, Francillon and Phillips managed to persuade the original subscribers (the Governors) to take the collection and agree to continue with the original commission, with the result that a further collection was bought by the library in 1809. The complaint seemed to centre on the style of the painting, and in particular on Abbot's use of miniature backgrounds of plants and sometime houses (in imitation of George Edwards's miniaturised scenic backgrounds), ensuring that the bird itself stood proud and erect.

The entire Chetham collection of bird paintings and notes was sold by auction in 1980 by Christie, Mason and Wood. It was broken up and subsequently sold on to museums, libraries, institutions and private collections, mostly in the United States.

As with the insect paintings, Abbot's birds were accompanied by notes indicating where they were to be found, whether they were migrants, and describing their general habitat. Specimens were carefully measured immediately after they were trapped or shot. The bird paintings are not numbered in the same way as the insect paintings, although it is clear from the various collections that Abbot did produce duplicates. Simpson (1984) has carefully collated the paintings in various collections, showing their similarities and listing those he regards as copies of Abbot paintings by other authors such as Latham and Wilson.

One of the largest individual collections of Abbot's watercolours of birds is in the British Library. The so called Egerton Manuscript comprises 295 watercolours of birds and eggs, accompanied by manuscript descriptions of the birds, with names and biological notes – all in Abbot's hand.[25] Abbot rarely dated his paintings, and although two volumes are dated 1804, there is no indication when the collection was started. Sawyer's (1949)

researches led him to believe that the 'Egerton Birds' were originally owned by John Dent FRS (died 1827). Dent's extensive library included a set of Abbot's paintings, and the whole was sold in 1827 at auction.[26] In 1845, the volumes of Abbot birds were bequeathed to the British Museum by Francis Egerton, Earl of Bridgewater, as part of the Egerton Manuscript collection. The paintings contain Latham's scientific names and references to Latham's publications (in a hand similar to Abbot's) suggesting that Abbot had access to them. The two men had corresponded and Abbot had sent Latham specimens and paintings, so it seems likely that Latham also sent Abbot a set of his books.

A Georgian physician, Joshua Elder White (fl. 1798–1820), who was a member of the Savannah Library Society, a friend of Abbot's and an ornithologist of some repute, commissioned from Abbot a set of watercolours of birds, which was to be accompanied by a catalogue. The set was finished in 1815 but by 1817 White had for some reason sold it complete to Lord Edward Smith Stanley, later the 13th Earl of Derby, for his library at Knowsley Hall, near Liverpool. Lord Stanley was a famous collector of natural history objects and memorabilia, who also had a large menagerie, He was to acquire both bird skins and paintings from Abbot, and Abbot's paintings are still in the library at Knowsley Hall.

John Abbot's interest lay not just in the spectacular butterflies and birds that were to be found in Georgia. Not even the feather lice of birds or the smallest spider escaped his notice, and for special customers such as Latham he even resorted to dissection. The total number of paintings that he made, or that are extant today, will probably never be known. The list that follows includes all the known holdings of Abbot paintings that I have been able to trace, but is probably far from complete.

PLATE 51 Ichneumon wasp, female *Megarhyssa atracta* (Fabricius) [*Ichneumon atratus* Fab.]

*Frequents oak woods and swamps very rare. They breed in stumps of trees that has been cut down. I have taken them when laying their eggs with their tails thrust into the wood so far that they were sometimes not able to disengage themselves.*

Plate size 12 × 20 cm. *Insects of Georgia* (Francillon), XII, p. [69], pl. 14

14.

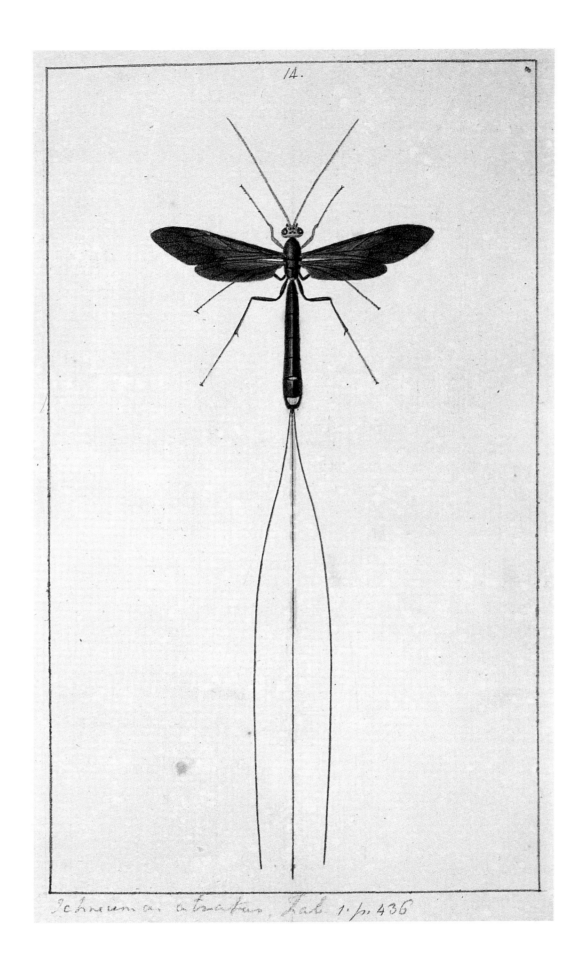

Ichneumon atratus. Fab 1. p. 436

NOTES

1 Wilkinson (1984).

2 Hellman (1948); Shoumatoff (1982).

3 Francillon to Phillips, British Library Add. Ms. 295433.

4 *Original papers (Natural history)* 7f. pp. 158–59, 5 February 1883, The Natural History Museum, London. Gunther's memorandum:

"The entomologist John Abbot lived in the second half of the last century, and devoted many years of his life to drawing the insects observed by him in the Southern States of North America. He drew them from fresh or living specimens in their natural colours which, in many species, fade after death or disappear in preserved examples. Of the thousands of species figured by him, many have not been rediscovered, and some at least, with the increase of population, seem to have disappeared entirely from the countries where they were common in Abbot's time. The perhaps most valuable portion of the collection is contained in the volumes treating of the transformation of Insects; some of these drawings have been reproduced in works published by Sir J.E. Smith, Boisduval and Le Conte, but these productions are so unsatisfactory, that many of them can only be determined by reference to the originals. [Gunther was mistaken – no watercolours from this set were published by the authors mentioned.]

"As a manuscript, the collection does not possess any value, the accompanying notes are, merely information on localities etc. as regards the specimens figured; as a work of art it is surpassed by others, notably Abbot's contemporary Rosel, who painted his insects on vellum. But it has a wider repute on account of its scientific value which as far as the North American Fauna is concerned, can hardly be over estimated. Therefore, it is constantly consulted in the Zoological Department, together with the specimens, in general as well as in special inquiries, and is of the greatest assistance whenever North American insects have to be arranged; and there is scarcely one among the North American Entomologists who has not written to the Zoological Department for information about species figured in Abbot.

"Whilst thus Abbot's drawings have been always used, and proved an essential aid, in connection with entomological work of the Department, the drawings by themselves would lose much of their value and usefulness, if they were placed beyond the means of comparing them with as nearly as perfect a collection of specimens as possible; because in many groups of insects the species are so closely allied that a comparison with specimens is necessary to ensure the correct identification of the drawings.

"Dr Gunther has been informed that Abbot's drawings are acquired by the Trustees from funds granted to the Department of Manuscripts.

If required, Dr Gunther would willingly give his consent to the cost being refunded to the Department from the grant made for the Zoological Department.

"The collection was made up as follows:

Vols. 1–4 Coleoptera 803 paintings

Vol. 5 Orthoptera, Homoptera and Hemiptera 289 paintings

Vol. 6 Lepidoptera – Rhopalocera 100 paintings

Vols. 7–11 Lepidoptera – Heterocera 616 paintings

Vol. 12 Neuroptera and Hymenoptera 277 paintings

Vol. 13 Diptera 273 paintings

Vol. 14 Arachnida 117 paintings

Vol. 15 Myriopoda, Mallophaga, Acarina, Crustacea, Lepidoptera (transformations) 20 paintings

Vol. 16 Portrait, Orthoptera, Coleoptera, Lepidoptera (transformations) 130 paintings

Vol. 17 Lepidoptera (transformations) 133 paintings"

5 A.H. Haworth, *Transactions of the Entomological Society*, I, London 1907, pp. 1–69.

6 Introductory note sent by Abbot to Smith about his illustrations for *The Natural History of the rarer Lepidopterous Insects of Georgia*, Linnean Society, London.

7 Swainson correspondence, Linnean Society, London.

8 Smith papers, Linnean Society, London.

9 R. Brooks, *A new system of natural history. 6 volumes fully illustrated*, 1763. This may be the work alluded to by Abbot, but I have not seen a coloured copy.

10 'A bookseller's latchpenny': something new and bright to attract customers.

11 E. Albin, British Museum, Sloane Ms. 3338, f. v.

12 *Proceedings of the Entomological Society, Washington*, no. 23, pp. 69–99.

13 Emory University, Atlanta, Georgia, purchased a set of Abbot paintings which included a charcoal drawing of a man wearing a tall hat and carrying around his neck what appears to be a tray of insects. There is a strong possibility that this may be another self-portrait of Abbot not previously published.

14 G. Edwards (1743–51), vol. I, introduction, p. xvii. Edwards had done all his own engraving. Catesby had encouraged him and "invited me to see him work at Etchings, and gave me all the necessary hints and instruction".

PLATE 52

90  *Epistenia* sp. [*Chrysis*]

*Taken 21st May settled on a dead limb of a tree in Briar Creek swamp. Very rare.*

92  ?*Torymus* sp. [*Chrysis*]

*Taken 28th March off a small pine in oak woods the only one I have seen.*

Plate size 13.5 × 19 cm. *Insects of Georgia* (Francillon), XII, p. [98], pl. +++90, +++92

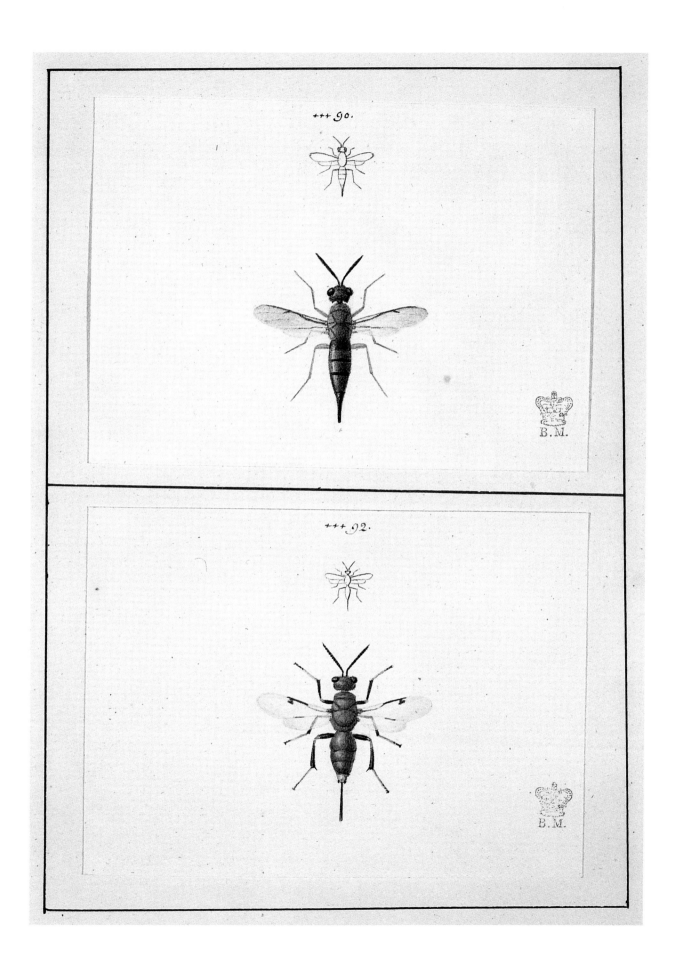

+++ *90.*

+++ *92.*

B.M.

B.M.

15  Dow (1914), p.71.

16  Abbot to T.W. Harris, 1835, Dow (1914).

17  Illustrators and engravers of Boisduval and Le Conte plates:

Plates 1, 22, 24–29 All drawn by Abbot (misspelt Abbott) and engraved by Duméril

Plates 23, 30 Drawn and engraved by Duméril

Plates 31–40, 42, 44, 46, 48, 49 Drawn by Abbot (spelt correctly) and engraved by Borromée

Plates 51, 53, 55–59, 61, 62 These and all the remaining plates engraved 64–74, 77, 78 by Borromée

Plates 41, 45, 47, 50, 52, 54, 60, 63, 75–76 Drawn by Blanchard

Plate 43 Drawn by Le Conte

18  Abbot to Swainson, 20 December 1816, Swainson correspondence, Linnean Society, London. In 1816, Abbot had written to Swainson, offering him numerous illustrations, and Swainson had agreed to take them.

19  Abbot to Swainson, 1835, Linnean Society, London.

20  Augustus Oemler, Abbot's friend in Savannah, had been instrumental in commissioning Abbot's collection of natural history paintings for the Savannah Library Society. A group of local enthusiasts had started the Society in 1809, Oemler among them.

21  Henry Mühlenberg, a plant collector and enthusiastic botanist, corresponded with Baldwin and others wishing to exchange plant specimens. Baldwin to Mühlenberg, 1811:

"I have looked over, with great pleasure, the interesting drawings of the amiable Mr Abbott. Those at the Library … executed under the inspection of Mr Oemler. They are as far as I am qualified for judging, exquisitly beautiful and scientifically accurate."

Baldwin to Mühlenberg, 1845:

"… at Savannah, you will have an opportunity to see that excellent man Mr Abbott, whose drawings of Georgia insects and Plants, are so justly admired, I wish to have your opinion on the new drawings he has made for the Library at Savannah."

22  Bibliothèque Centrale du Muséum National d'Histoire Naturelle, Paris, Mss. 841 and 274.

23  Francillon to Phillips, British Library, Add Ms. 295433.

24  Francillon to Phillips, British Library, Add Ms. 295433:

"I have sent you 90 drawings of insects etc from Mr John Abbot of Savannah at 8/6 each for your Gentleman of the Manchester Library inspection upon sale or return."

Francillon to Phillips, British Library, Add Ms. 295433:

"… 90 drawings of insects and their plants returned by the Gentleman of Manchester Library … for notwithstanding they have Dr Smith's work. They can only have the number which they have at present and never any addition to it, unless they take these drawings … and take the remainder as Mr Abbot will complete them … in about two years."

25  British Museum, Egerton Mss. 1137, 1138.

26  Dent sale catalogue, lot 108:

"Abbot's American Birds. A most beautiful assemblage of highly coloured drawings of the Birds of Georgia in America, accompanied with descriptions, and the Latin, English and Georgian names in manuscript, collected and painted from life by John Abbot of Savannah many years resided in that country. 2 vols splendidly bound in Green Morocco by Lewis, gilt leaves. This unique collection of original [drawings] consisting of 246 highly finished figures was executed purposely for the late Mr Francillon who commissioned the Artist to send him accurate portraits of all the Birds of Georgia which he could obtain from living subjects. This has been faithfully executed and the collection has been submitted to the judgement of that able ornithologist Dr Latham who has named such as is known, the rest are non-descript, and have not hitherto been made public in any shape."

PLATE 53 *Asilus proctoacanthus* Macquart

*Taken 12th June in Oak and Pine Woods. This genus are called in Savannah Wolf Flies in general, and by many people Witches. They are as great devourers of other Insects as the Libellula. It is curious to observe them when they have caught one of the Hymenoptera class, to see them hold it out at arms length (as it were) while they continue sucking its blood, till they render the Insects too weak to be stung by them, they likewise prey on every kind of their own Genus (Wolf Fly) that they are able to conquer. Common.*

Plate size 10 × 15.5 cm. *Insects of Georgia* (Francillon), XIII, p. [72], pls. 73 and 74

73.

74.

*asilus*

*19.*

*Stratyomys.*

B.M.

PLATE 54  *Stratyomys* – Syrphidae, *Microdon sp.* [*Musca*]
*Taken 2nd July in Oak and Pine Woods. Rare.*

Plate size 12 × 18 cm. *Insects of Georgia* (Francillon), XIII, p. [36], pl. 19


PLATE 55

No. 111  *Physoconops bulbirostris* Loew [*Conops*]
*Taken 20th July on blossoms in Oak and Pine Woods. Not very common.*
No. 112. *Physoconops picta* Fab. [*Conops*]
*Taken 14th May. frequents blossoms in Oak and Pine woods. Not very common.*

Plate size 12 × 18 cm. *Insects of Georgia* (Francillon), XIII, p. [66], pls. 111 and 112

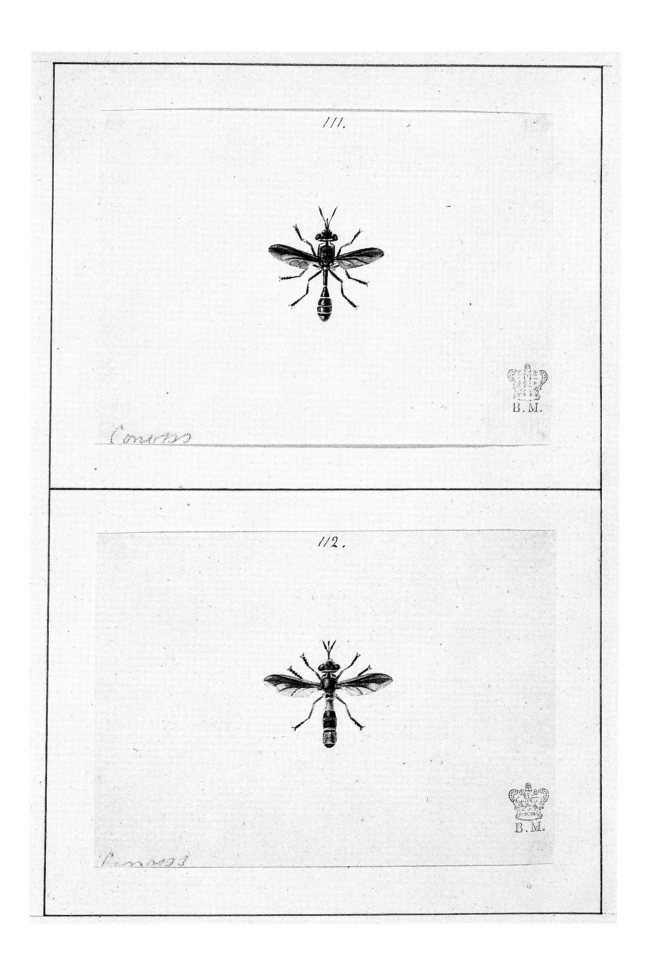

111.

Conops

112.

Conops

113

# Known Locations of Original Abbot Watercolours and Specimens

## Watercolours

Alexander Turnbull Library, Wellington, New Zealand

American Philosophical Society, Philadelphia

Amon Carter Museum, Fort Worth, USA

Atlanta Historical Society, Atlanta GA

British Museum, London, UK

Chethams Library, Manchester, UK: collection sold at auction in 1980 by Christie, Manson & Woods Ltd, London, broken up and sold on to private collectors, museums and galleries

Corcoran Gallery of Art, Washington DC

Lord Derby Collection, Knowsley Hall, Liverpool

Emory University, School of Medicine, Department of Medicine, Atlanta GA

Emory University Special Collections, Robert W. Woodruff Library

University of Georgia Library, Special Collections, Atlanta GA

Houghton Library, Harvard University, Cambridge MA

John Works Garrett Collections, Milton S. Eisenhower Library, Johns Hopkins University: original paintings for Smith and Abbot 1797

The Natural History Museum, London

University of North Carolina at Chapel Hill, Rare Books Collections

Academy of Natural Sciences, Philadelphia

University of South Carolina, Columbia, Thomas Cooper Library

Smithsonian Institution, Washington DC

Bibliothèque Centrale du Muséum National d'Histoire Naturelle, Paris

Statesboro Regional Library

Tall Timbers Research Station, Talahassee

Many watercolours are also known to be held in private hands in the USA.

Some of the early literature on Abbot indicates that collections of Abbot watercolours existed in Switzerland and possibly in other European countries. I have not been able to establish the home of any such collections. It is possible that some were destroyed in World War II, or that collections have not been identified as being by Abbot.

## Specimens

County Museum Department, Merseyside County Council, Liverpool: bird skins from Lord Derby's collection

Zoological Museum, Berlin, Germany: remains of a larger original collection of bird skins; many specimens were destroyed during the bombing in World War II

Kirby (1888) and Horn *et al.* (1990) indicate that insect specimens are extant in the collections of The Natural History Museum, London, and the Museum of Science and Arts, Dublin; I have not been able to establish this with any certainty; they may have been incorporated into the general American collections

Museum of Comparative Zoology, Harvard University, USA: bird skins

Charleston Museum: plant specimens sent to Elliott by Abbot as part of a larger herbarium collection

---

PLATE 56  *Carabus sycophanta*

*Taken 16th April in the body of an Oak in Ogechee Swamps. Likewise sometimes found in oak woods of Virginia where I have taken them eating the chrysalis of the oak hockey moth. Common in Virginia.*

Plate size 11 × 14 cm. *Insects of Georgia* (Francillon), V, p. [28], pl. 402

402.

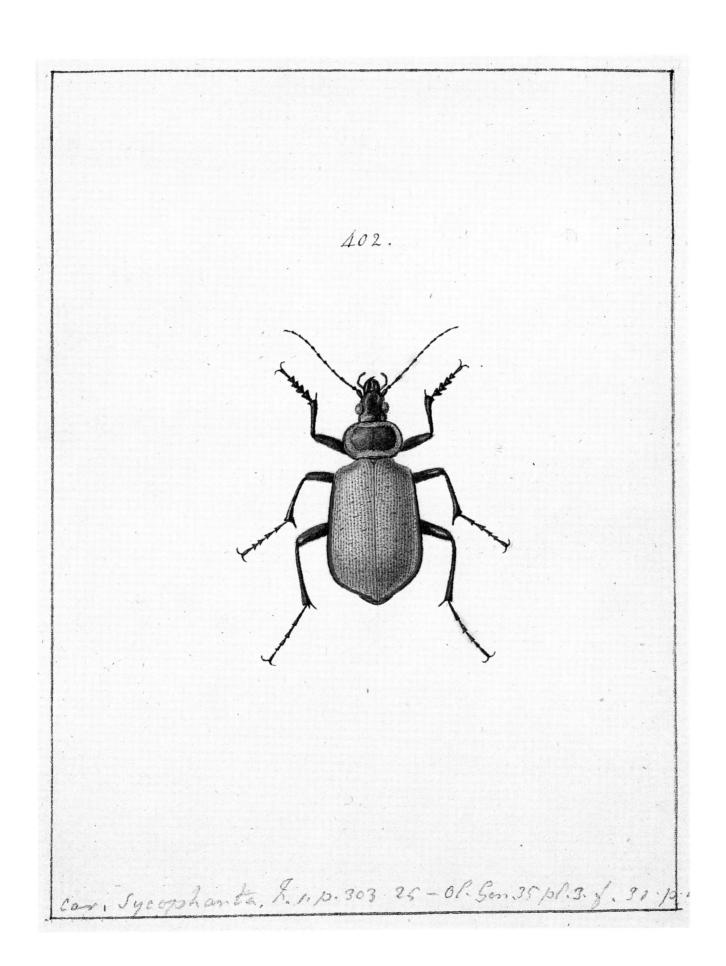

Car. Sycophanta. L. i. p. 303. 25 – Ol. Gen 35 pl. 3. f. 31. p.

1.

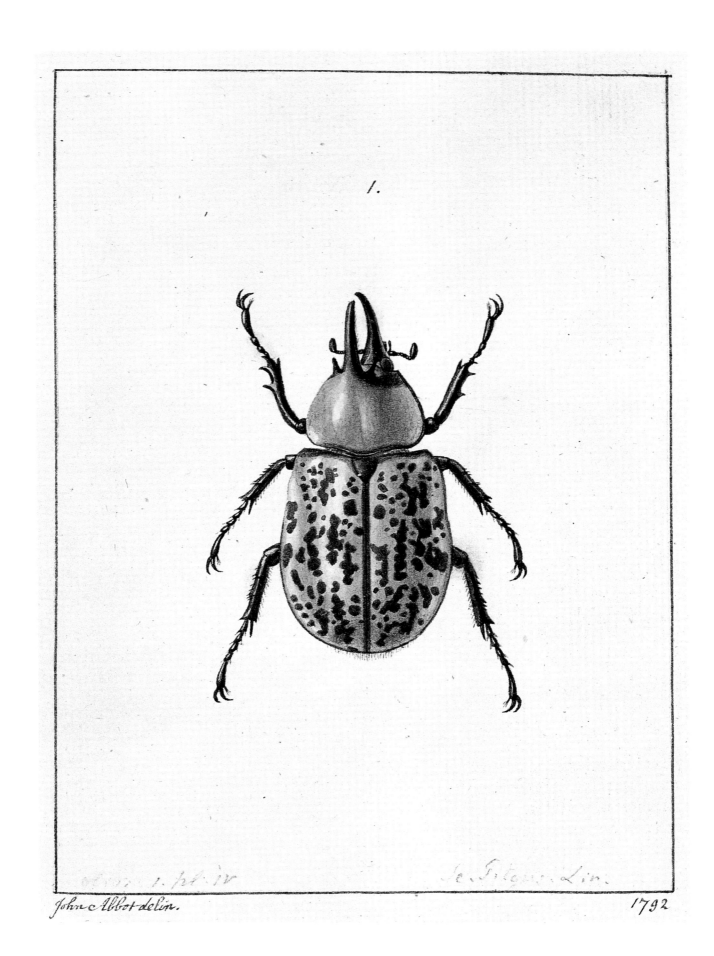

1792

116

# 'Notes on my Life'

PLATE 57 Scarab beetle *Dynastes tityus* (Linn.) [Elephant Beetle, *Scarabaeus Tityus*]

*The larva of this Sarabaeus differs little, except in size some feeds in the inside of decayed trees, and Earth that is rich with some manure, or Dung, it breeds in Oaks, Flys in the night and sometimes enters houses, it is scarce particularly the male. Taken about the 25th of May and as late as the 6th Oct. It is found likewise in Virginia. After they are dead they change black and in a year or two (when dry) they recover their color again. This sooner happens when exposed to the sun. Commonly called in Georgia Elephant Beetle.*

*Signed John Abbot delin. 1792.*

Plate size 11 × 14 cm. *Insects of Georgia* (Francillon), I, p. [1], pl. 1

I was born in the year 1751, the first of June the Old Stile at the West end of the Town London, in Bennet Street St. James, my father was an Attorney at Law, I was his 2d Son my brother dying before I was born, at the time of my leaving England I had 2 sisters, Elizabeth & Charlotte, and a brother Thomas then seven years old. I had an early love for Books laying out my pocket money for little Story books, and an early taste for drawing, which might be much increased by my father having a large & valuable collection of prints, of some of the best Masters, he had also many good paintings.

My peculiar liking for Insects was long before I was acquainted with any method of catching or keeping them – I remember knocking down a Libella and pining it, when I was told it would sting, as bad as a Rattle snake bite.

My Father had a Country house, at Turnham Green 5 miles from London at £25 a year rent, at the early part of my Life, I remember breeding some there, when I had no method of keeping them after I had done it. When the Lease expired my father gave it up as the grounds and house was devided, between the heirs of it. I have a drawing of the house, which I will send you some time hence.

In one of my Walks after Insects I met with a Mr Van Dest the famous flower painter, he invited me to come and see him, he had been a small Collector, showed me a pattern of the large Net & gave me some rare insects, I got me immediately a Net made & began to understand keeping them better.

My father got a Mr Bonneau an Engraver & Drawing Master, to give me lessons of Drawing at our own house, he was acquainted with a Mr Rice a Teacher of Grammer, who had likewise been a Collector of Insects, Mr Bonneau, did not paint in Water Colours, he only understood the Rules of Drawing and perspective, he praised my Drawings of Insects, & got me, through Mr Rice introduced to Mr Drury who had been president of the Linnean Society & who then was allowed to have the best Collection of Insects both English and foreign of any one.

I leave you to judge my pleasure and astonishment at the sight of his cabinets the first I had ever seen of the kind he very politely offered to lend me insects to Draw,

& we immediately became well acquainted. That hour may be said to have given a new turn to my future life. I had immediately a Mahogony Cabinet made of 26 drawers, covered with sliding tops of glass, it cost me 6 Guineas, & began to collect with an increasing industry. I met with, and soon after purchased a parcel of beautiful Insects from Surinam. I soon began to have a respectable collection but not satisfied with it I craved more.

One day a Mr Smeathman a young Man introduced himself to me, by saying he understood by Mr Rice, I was a brother Flycatcher, and had come to see me, I am not fond of strangers, but his Address & discourse, soon settled an immediate acquaintance, he has a small collection, among them an English Purple Emperor, it is rare, I never met with any myself, I gave him a Guinea for it. On the other hand in one of my walks, I met with a hornet Moth, not larger than a hornet, a Gentleman offered me 2 Guineas for it, I thought the offer so liberal I let him have it, I also sold my duplicate English Insects at a good price. This Mr Smeathman went to Africa on an intention chiefly to collect insects, he stayed 2 or 3 years, & returned to England after I left it, he made a publication on it, particular on account of the Ants, and the large hillocks they make there, he was going out there again, as Deputy Governor, to a British Establishment there, but was taken with a fever and died.

I now began to entertain thoughts of going abroad to collect foreign insects myself.

I had bought Albins history of the changes of Insects coloured which was great use to me, he had also published 3 vols of Birds – my father went to purchase it, at an Auction of Books, but did not & instead bought 4 vols of Mr Edwards Birds, but so much superior to Albins, I was much pleased with the change, but there was 3 more to be published later, we went together to his house to buy them. I carried some of my Drawings with me, he praised them much and desired me by all means to continue Drawing, saying no doubt I would be a publisher hereafter of some work on Natural history.

About this time Lady Honeywood, widow of General Honeywood made me a present of Catesby's Nat. Hist. of Carolina a subscription Copy £20 price, all this you may suppose increased my love in general for Nat. history.

I was articled to my Father as his Clerk for 5 years to be an Attorney, but Deeds, Conveyances and Wills etc. was but little to my 1iking when my thoughts was engrosed by Natural History.

In the beginning of the year 1773, I was determined to come to America, but what part to choose was the only matter to determine on. A Frenchman & his son come from Orleans, they praised that very much, but I had met with a hist of Virginia painted in such glowing Colours, & the Voyage there being much shorter I determined on Virginia. I sold my Cabinet of Insects, drawings etc. I had 3 smaller Wainscot Cabinets made to bring with me and engaged my passage in the Royal Exchange, Cpt. Woodford the Ship had undergone a thorough Repair and was to sail in April, but through delays did not sail untill July. In the summer thro' the

PLATE 58

*19* Dung beetle *Phanaeus vindex* Macleay [*Scarabaeus Carnifax*]

*Taken in all the warm months in the year. It flys in the Day time in search of excrements newly fallen from Man or Beasts. They form balls of it in which they deposit their Eggs, these they roll with their breach backwards into deep holes, which they make under or near the dung.*

*20 Female of the former called in Georgia Tumble (T-d) Dung*

*21 The Thorax of this is always of a more beautiful colour than the 2 former, which is often entirely green, the female of this species also differs in shape of the breast from the other. It is found with the former but is more frequent in the autumn.*

Plate size 11 × 16 cm. *Insects of Georgia* (Francillon), I, p. [38], pls. 19–21

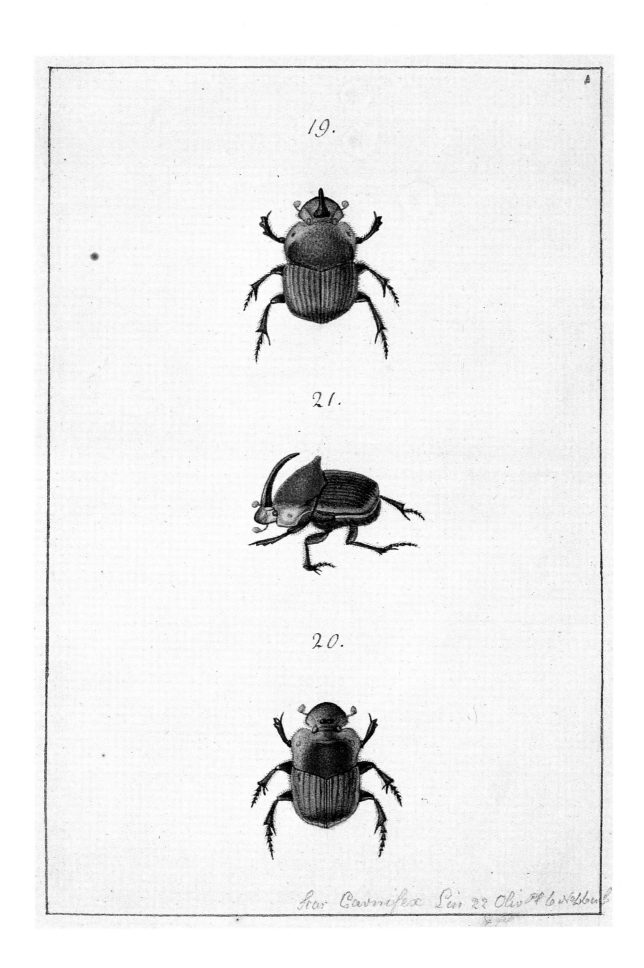

19.

21.

20.

Scar Carnifex Lin 22 Oliv n° 6 Nebbu

recommendation of a Mr Humphreys I was employed in making Drawings of Nat. history shells etc. at a good price, on Vellum at a guinea a piece. A gentleman I drawed for prersuaded me delay my departure & draw for him but it was to late.

One Morning I went to the Coffee house to know when the Ship would sale, was told she had sailed, but might perhaps overtake her in the River, before she got out to Sea.

*To be continued in my next letter*

Notes on my Life continued

I was a good deal surprised and alarmed, I had paid for my passage 25 Guineas and my clothes and baggage was on board.

I hired a post chaise & in Company with my father & mother & my brother Tommy then 7 years old, we started to overtake the Ship before it got out of the River to Sea, Uppon a point of land on the River we got in sight of the Ship, but far ahead, all the chance was then to go to Deal on the sea coast, from whence She was to take her final Departure.

Upon our arrival at Deal we saw with pleasure the Ship lying off, which had got there before us, I immediately hired a boat and got on board her. I took leave of my Mother in tears, but my brother Tommy pleased with his Tour I suppose said he was sorry I was going to leave him, but hang him if he could cry.

The Ship did not sail till 3 days after, the wind not being fair, the Captain & some of the passengers next day went on shore, but I was determinded to stay on board as I had got there. There was 8 Cabin Passengers of us — among them was a Mr Goodall & his Wife an English woman who he had married during his stay in England, he was furrnished by his Uncle a rich Merchant in London England, with a cargo of Goods to set up a store in Virginia in Hanover County where he lived,

about 100 miles from the mouth of the James River.

In about a fortnight we got to Madeira, where we stop a day or two to take in some Wine. I landed there walked about the Town & dined at a hotel. Altho it was a fine day I did not meet with any Butterfly or Moth.

About the 9th Sept. we made James River & anchored near the mouth, being 6 weeks on the Passage.

I had a Letter of Recommendation from Mr Drury to a Minister in Dinwiddee County, but I had commenced an Acquaintance with Mr Goodall and with his consent agreed to board with him the Parson being a total stranger & living still much further back in the country.

Mr Goodall got acquainted with a Mr Balfour who had a small Sloop & was going up James River on a commission to buy up a large quantity of Wheat to ship to England, he very politely offered to carry us up the River as far as Old James Town, the first settlement in Virginia.

Upon my landing there I found it was now deserted as a Town, we there hired 2 chairs, one for myself & the other for Mr Goodall & his Wife, with an Attendant who was to bring them back again.

Soon after my arrival at Mr Goodalls it became very sickly in the neighbourhood, with fevers & fluxes, one of Mr Goodalls Negroes died of the Flux, and many of the neighbours; in one family 22 died in 2 years white and black leaving only a little Girl heir to the Estate.

I was very fortunate in not being sick at all during my 2 years stay in Virginia, and escaping a seasoning to the Country & it was not till the 2nd year in Georgia before I had the Ague & fever.

During the next Summer I was much disappointed in not meeting the variety of insects I expected, I was likewise very unlucky, I shipped a Cabinet of Insects for London, but the Ship was lost on the English coast, together with my insects. I got much dispirited, & come to the resolution to return to England again, the times

PLATE 59 Great dung beetle *Dichotomius carolinus* Linn. [*Scarabaeus carolinus* Linn.]
*It flies in the evening, often enters House, burys itself under Cow Dung to the depth of a foot in the earth. Taken in May, often found much later. Commonly called in Georgia the Great Dung Beetle.*

Plate size 11 × 14 cm. *Insects of Georgia* (Francillon), I, p. [6], pl. 7

7.

*Scar Carolinus Luis 16. Oliv.* 12 113

likewise becoming alarming. I was told that a Captain of a Ship bound for London was to be at the Court House, I went there with Mr Goodall but the Captain was not coming, I gave it out.

In the mean time I got acquainted with one William Goodall, a cousin to the former a young man who had lived in Georgia, with his Relations, but who had married in Virginia he talked much in Praise of Georgia, and wanted to go back there but had not the means to bear his Expenses.

The Colinies having appointd a day after which all Intercourse with England, was to be stopped I fixed up another Cabinet of Insects to send to England, they was on board the boat on the River to the Ship, when a terrible September storm arose in the night, and the boat was lost together with my insects again, but to make me amends I have not lost any I have sent from Georgia.

The times now becoming very troublesome, & hearing that Georgia had not joined the other coIinies, I joined Wm Goodall to come to Georgia together. I furnished 2 horses & was to bear all our Expenses, he & one cart to carry his wife & child & a little negro boy & our baggage.

Thus fixed we started one day early in Dcr., accompanied by a Cousin of his who lived in North Carolina, I must confess I parted my Virginia friends with some regret. I felt much more depressed in my mind for some hours than when I left England.

When we got to the Tar River N.C. we stopped at his Uncles where we was entertained & rested ourselves a week. We continued our Journey, & early one day conversing with a man that lived on the Road, he found out that it was a cousin of his, we were then invited to stay till next day. We continued on to Roanoke River, the ferry was kept by one Sproles an Irishman, the cold set

in so severe that we could not cross the River for the ice for sevl days, Sproles out of regard for my being a countryman only charged us 14 shilling C. currency for houseroom, the snow also lay deep on the road & the next night after crossing the River, had to scrape away the snow to lay our beds down by a light wood fire, but still slept comforatbly.

*To be continued*

Continuation of my Notes

Early the next morning as we travelled the road forked and not unluckably we took the wrong one, we soon came to a deserted store & out buildings, we immediately took up camp & stayed about a week till the snow melted and the weather cleared up, we obtained here, being near a Scotch Settlement, some fresh provisions, & some good Cyder. Thus refreshed, with fresh Spirits we got again into our direct road, & travelled for 2 or 3 days more, in the evening we came to a house on the road, it was very cold, & our horses had performed a good days travel, we was very desirous to take up, it was kept by an old woman, her son, & 2 or 3 daughters, the old Woman would not let us stay, she said it was but 2 miles to another house where we might stay — her son and daughters entreated for us, but the old hag was enexorable, we had to travel full five miles more, we stopped, had a good fire & supper, to make amends for our late nights travel. We traveled on to Dee dee River, here Wm Goodall had another cousin an Overseer to a large plantation. We stayed here 2 or 3 days, I had now got a bad cold, but upon taking some stewed liquor, it cured it, & then continued our Journey on the road to Augusta we crossed the ferry, & Wm Goodall sent word from Augusta by some persons he knew, for Wm Moore his brother in law & Pleasant Goodall his half-brother, to meet us next day with fresh horses, which they did, and about

PLATE 60 [Black Cerambyx]

*The caterpillar feeds in small or young Hickory roots (called here Grub) and oak grubs. It changed into chrysalis in a cavity it had made in the root June 10th and bred 29th June. It is frequently found in Oak Woods and corn fields the latter end of June and July.*

Plate size 23 × 30 cm. *Insects of Georgia* (Rothschild bequest), I, pl. 2

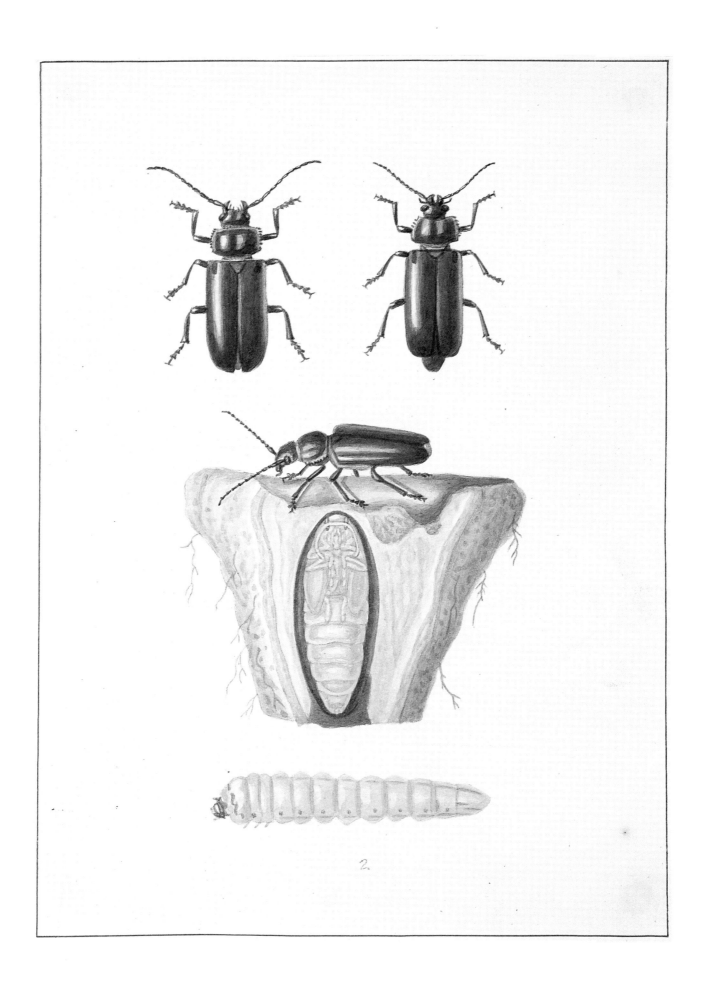

2.

dinner time got to Wm Moores house, about 30 miles below August about the beginning of February, performing our Journey in about 2 months, in the middle of winter, but I arrived in good health and spirits, had seen a good deal of the Country, and many amusing passing scenes. We took up our abode with Pleasant Goodall who then kept bachelors house, till a house could be built of logs for Wm Goodall, on a part adjoining of Wm. Moores land. When that was finished we moved there, and I took up my board with him for some time after.

I was now settled in Georgia for a season I might now take leave of my notes, but as the first years of my living in Georgia, contains much more of Adventure, than the former part of my life, and continued through such bad & terrible time, that I often reflect ,upon the goodness of providence, in bringing me safely through them.

When I am again settled I will continue with them, with the many curious Anecdotes of the Times. Indeed I often think if I had the Genius of a Scot or Bulwar, to colour some parts highly, and some occasional additions, it might make an amusing Novel of 2 vols.

*John Abbot*

# Bibliography

ANON., Francillon death notice, *The Gentleman's Magazine*, **86** (2), 1816, p. 92

ANON., *Encyclopedia Britannica*, **7** (Macropaedia), 1978, pp. 1125–27

ANON., *History of the collections contained in the Natural History Departments of the British Museum*, I: *The Libraries*, London (British Museum: Natural History) 1904

ANON., *History of Insects*, (Religious Tract Society), 1842

ABBOT, J., *Insects of Georgia*, 17 vols. of watercolours, unpublished

ABBOT, J., *Insects of Georgia*, 2 vols. of watercolours, unpublished (part of Rothschild bequest)

ABBOT, J., *Moths of Georgia*, 2 vols. of watercolours, unpublished

ABBOT, J., *Birds of Georgia, consisting of the most rare and beautiful birds*, watercolours, unpublished (part of Rothschild bequest)

ALBIN, E., *A Natural History of English Insects*, London 1720

ALBIN, E., *A Natural History of Birds*, 3 vols., London 1738

ALLEN, D.E., 'Joseph Dandridge and the first Aurelian Society', *Entomologist's Record and Journal of Variation*, **78**, 1966, pp. 89–94

ALLEN, D.E., 'John Martyn's Botanical Society; a biographical analysis of the membership', *Proceedings of the Botanical Society of the British Isles*, **6**, 1967, pp. 305–24

ALLEN, D.E., *The Naturalist in Britain, a social history*, London (Allen Lane) 1976

ALLEN, D.E., 'Natural History in Britain in the eighteenth century', *Archives of Natural History*, **20**, 1993, pp. 333–47

ALLEN, E.G., 'A third set of John Abbot's drawings', *Auk*, **59**, 1942, pp. 563–71

ALLEN, E.G., 'A resumé of John Abbot's *Notes on my Life*', *Oriole*, **13**, 1948, pp. 31–32

ALLEN, E.G., 'History of American Ornithology before Audubon', *Transactions of the American Philosophical Society*, **41**, 1951, pp. 386–591

ALLEN, E.G., 'John Abbot, pioneer naturalist of Georgia', *Georgia Historical Quarterly*, **41**, 1957, pp. 143–57

ALLINGHAM, E.G., *A romance of the rostrum*, London (Witherby) 1924

APPERSON, G.L., *Bygone London Life, Pictures from a Vanished Past*, London (Elliot Stock) 1903

ARMITAGE, A., 'A naturalist's vacation: the letters of J.C. Fabricius', *Annals of Science*, **14**, 1958, pp. 116–31

BAKER, W.B., 'John Abbot's Insects of Georgia', *Emory University Quarterly*, **15**, 1959, pp. 146–52

BANISTER, J., 'The extracts of Four Letters from Mr. John Banister to Dr Lister communicated by him to the Publisher', *Philosophical Transactions of the Royal Society*, **18**, 1693, pp. 667–72

BASSETT, A.S., 'Some Georgia Records of John Abbot naturalist', *Auk*, **55**, 1938, pp. 242–54

BATES, R.S., *Scientific Societies in the United States*, 3rd edn., New York (Pergamon Press) 1965

BEIRNE, B.P., 'Some original paintings by John Abbot', *The Lepidopterists' Society*, **4**, 1950, pp. 25–26

BENEZIT, E., *Dictionnaire critique et documentaire des peintres, sculpteurs, dessinateurs et graveurs*, **2**, Paris 1948–55, p. 3

BRASCH, F.E. , 'The Royal Society of London and its influence upon scientific thought in the American Colonies', *Scientific Monthly*, **33**, 1931, pp. 197–201, 336–469

BRENNAN, M.T. and MORGAN, P.J., 'Lord Edward Smith Stanley (1775–1851), 13th Earl of Derby. A review of his biological collections and their importance', *Biology Curators' Group Newsletter*, **1**, 1977, pp. 20–28

BRISTOWE, W.S., 'The life of the great English naturalist Joseph Dandridge (1664–1746)', *Entomologists' Gazette*, **18**, 1967, pp. 73–89

BULLOCK, W., *A Companion to Mr Bullock's Museum and Pantherion*, 12th edn., London 1812

CANTWELL, R., *Alexander Wilson: Naturalist and Pioneer*, Philadelphia (J.B. Lippincott Co.) 1961

CARTER, H.B., *Sir Joseph Banks (1743–1920)*, London (British Museum: Natural History) 1988

CATESBY, M., *The Natural History of Carolina, Florida and the Bahamas*, 2 vols, London 1731–43

CATESBY, M., 1997. See McBurney, H.

CHALMERS-HUNT, J.M., *Natural History Collections 1700–1972: A register of sales in the British Isles*, London (Sotheby/Park Bernet) 1976

CHAMBERLAIN, R.V., and IVIE, W., 'John Abbot and the spiders of Georgia', *Bulletin of the University of Utah (Biological Services)*, **35**, 1944, pp. 7–24

COCKERELL, T.D.A., 'Dru Drury, an eighteenth-century entomologist', *Scientific Monthly*, **14**, 1922, pp. 67–82

COOLIDGE, H.V., *Four naturalists and their drawings of American Birds*, Georgia (Georgia Historical Society) 1970

COULTER, E.M., *Georgia: a short history*, Chapel Hill (University of North Carolina Press) 1960

COWAN, C.F., 'Boisduval and Le Conte: Histoire générale et Iconographie des Lépidoptères et des Chenilles de l'Amérique septentrionale', *Journal of the Society for the History of Natural History*, **5**, 1969, pp. 125–34

COWAN, C.F., 'John Francillon FLS. A few facts', *Entomologists' Record and Journal of Variation*, **98**, 1989, pp. 139–43

DARLINGTON, W., *Reliquiae Baldwinianae: Selections from the correspondence of the late William Baldwin MD*, Philadelphia 1843, pp. 50–57

DOW, R.P., 'John Abbot of Georgia', *Journal of the New York Entomological Society*, **22**, 1914, pp. 65–72

DREWETT, F.G.D., *The romance of the Apothecaries' Garden at Chelsea*, London (Chapman and Dodd) 1928

DRURY, D., *Letter Book, 1761–69*, Special Collections, Entomology Library of The Natural History Museum, London

DRURY, D., *Illustrations of Natural History*, 3 vols., London 1770–82

DRURY, D., *Thoughts on the precious metals, particularly gold; its general dissemination over the face of the globe with directions and hints to travellers, captains of ships, from the rough diamond down to the pebble*, London 1801

EDWARDS, G., *A Natural History of Uncommon Birds*, 4 vols., London 1743–51

EDWARDS, G., *Gleanings of Natural History*, 3 vols., London 1758–64

EDWARDS, W.H., *The Butterflies of North America*, I, New York (Houghton Mifflin & Co.) 1879–97

EWAN, J. and N., 'John Lyon: Nurseryman and plant hunter, his journal 1799–1814', *Transactions of the American Philosophical Society* (new series), **52** (2), 1963, pp. 5–69

FAULKNER, T., *An historical and topographical description of Chelsea and its environs*, 2 vols., London 1829

FAXON, W., 'John Abbot's drawings of the Birds of Georgia', *Auk*, **13**, 1896, pp. 204–15

FITTON, M. and GILBERT, P., 'Insect Collections', in MacGregor, A. (1994)

GOODE, G.B., 'The beginnings of Natural History in America' (Presidential address of the 6th anniversary meeting of the Biological Society of Washington), reprinted in *Annual Report of the Board of Regents of the US National Museum (2)*, 1897, 1901, pp. 357–406

GRAVES, A., *The Royal Academy of Arts: A complete dictionary of contributors*, 1, London 1905–06, p. 237

GRAVES, A., *The Society of Artists of Great Britain, 1760–91. The Free Society of Artists, 1761–83. A complete dictionary of contributors and their work from the foundation of the Societies to 1791*, London (George Bell & Sons) 1907

GREEN, J.C., *American Science in the age of Jefferson*, Ames (Iowa State University Press) 1984

GRIFFIN, F.J., 'Henry Smeathman (?–1786)', *Proceedings of the Royal Entomological Society of London (A)*, 17, 1942, pp. 1–9

GUNTHER, A.C.L.G., 'President's Address: The unpublished correspondence of William Swainson with contemporary naturalists (1806–1840) lately acquired by the Society', *Proceedings of the Linnean Society of London*, 112, 1900, pp. 14–61

HAGEN, H., 'Abbot's Handzeichnungen im Britischen Museum, und die Neuroptera Georgiens', *Stettiner Entomologische Zeitung*, 24, 1863, pp. 369–78

HARRIS, L., *Butterflies of Georgia*, Norman (University of Oklahoma Press) 1972

HELLMAN, G.T., 'Black tie and cyanide jar', *New Yorker*, 24, 1948, pp. 32–47

HINDLE, B., *The pursuit of science in Revolutionary America, 1735–1789*, Chapel Hill (University of North Carolina Press) 1956

HODLER, T.W., and SCHRETTER, H.A., *The Atlas of Georgia*, Athens (University of Georgia) 1986

HOPE, T.W., 'J.C. Fabricius' (translation from Danish autobiography, 1819), *Transactions of the Entomological Society of London*, 4 (suppl.), 1845, pp. 1–16

HORN, W., KAHLE, I., FRIESE, G. and GAEDIKE, R., *Collectiones entomologicae: Ein Kompendium über den Verbleib entomologischer Sammlungen der Welt bis 1960*, Eberswalde (Institut Pflanzenschutzforschung Kleinmachnow) 1990

HUGHES, A.F.N., *The American biologist through four centuries*, Illinois (C.C. Thomas) 1982

HULTON, P., and QUINN, D.B., *The American drawings of John White 1577–1590 with drawings of European and oriental subjects*, 2 vols., London (British Museum) 1964

HUNTER, C. (ed.), *The life and letters of Alexander Wilson*, Philadelphia (American Philosophical Society) 1983

INGLIS-JONES, E., *Peacocks in Paradise*, London (Faber and Faber) 1950

JARDINE, N., SECORD, J.A., and SPARY, E.C. (edd.), *Cultures of Natural History*, Cambridge (Cambridge University Press) 1996

JARDINE, W., 'John Abbot', *Naturalists' Library*, 32 (Exotic Moths), 1841, pp. 69–71

JESSOP, L., 'The Club at the Temple Coffee House – fact and supposition', *Archives of Natural History*, 16, 1989, pp. 263–74

JONES, W., 'The vogue of natural history in England, 1750–1806', *Annals of Science*, 2, 1937, pp. 345–52

KIRBY, W.F., 'John Abbot, the Aurelian', *Annual Report of the Entomological Society of Ontario*, 19, 1888, pp. 50–51. Also published in *Canadian Entomologist*, 20, pp. 230–32

LANDWEHR, J., *Studies in Dutch books with coloured plates, 1662–1875; natural history, topography and travel, costumes and uniforms*, The Hague (Junk) 1976

LARGEN, M.J., and ROGERS-PRICE, V., 'John Abbot, an early naturalist-artist in North America: his contribution to ornithology, with particular reference to a collection of bird skins in the Merseyside County Museum, Liverpool', *Archives of Natural History*, 12, 1985, pp. 231–52

LARSEN, A., 'Equipment for the field', in Jardine, N. *et al.* (1996), pp. 358–77

LECONTE, J., and BOISDUVAL, J.A., *Histoire générale et iconographie des lépidoptères et des chenilles de l'Amérique septentrionale*, Paris (Méquigon-Marvis) 1829–34

LISNEY, A.A., *Bibliography of British Lepidoptera, 1608–1799*, London (Chiswick Press) 1960

MACGREGOR, A. (ed.), *Sir Hans Sloane. Collector, Scientist, Antiquary, Founding father of the British Museum*, London (British Museum Press) 1994

MACKECHNIE-JARVIS, C., 'A History of British Coleoptera', *Proceedings of the British Entomological and Natural History Society*, 8, 1976 pp. 91–112

MACKECHNIE-JARVIS, C., 'John Francillon FLS, further facts', *Entomologists' Record and Journal of Variation*, 99, 1990, pp. 145–46

MCATEE, W.L., 'Georgian Records in John Latham's General History of Birds, 1821–1824', *Oriole*, 11, 1946, pp. 1–11

MCATEE, W.L., 'The date of Abbot's bird plates in the De Renne Collection', *Auk*, 67, 1950, p. 248

MCBURNEY, H., *Mark Catesby's Natural History of America*, London (Merrell Holberton) 1997

MALLIS, A., *American Entomologists*, New Brunswick (Rutgers University Press) 1971

MARTYN, T., *Psyche: figures of non-descript Lepidopterous insects or rarer moths and butterflies from different parts of the world*, London 1797

MATHEWS, G.M., 'John Latham (1740–1837): an early English Ornithologist', *Ibis* (13) 1, 1931, pp. 466–75

NEWMAN, E., *The Grammar of Entomology (Part 4): Preservation of insects*, London (F. Westley & A.H. Davis) 1835, pp. 261–303

NICHOLS, J., *Illustrations of the literary history of the eighteenth century*, 1, 1817, (letter, Sherard to Richardson re Dandridge) p. 359

NOBLETT, W., 'Dru Drury, his *Illustrations of Natural History* (1770–82) and the European market for printed books', *Quaerendo*, 15, 1985, pp. 83–102

NOBLETT, W., 'Dru Drury's *Directions for collecting insects in foreign countries*', *Bulletin of the Amateur Entomologists' Society*, 44, 1985, pp. 170–78

NOBLETT, W., 'Publishing by the author. A case study of Dru Drury's *Illustrations of Natural history* (1770–1782)', *Publishing History*, 23, 1988, pp. 67–94

OLESON, A., and BROWN, S.C. (edd.), *The pursuit of knowledge in the early American Republic. American scientific and learned societies from Colonial times to the Civil War*, Baltimore (The Johns Hopkins University Press) 1976

OSBORN, H., *A brief History of Entomology*, Columbus, Ohio (Spahr and Glenn) 1952

PARKINSON, P.G., 'Natural history drawings and watercolours by John Abbot, 'The Aurelian'' naturalist of Georgia, in the Alexander Turnbull Library', *Turnbull Library Record*, 11, 1978, pp. 26–36

PETIVER, J., 'Some observations concerning insects made by John Banister in Virginia, AD 1680', *Philosophical Transactions of the Royal Society*, 22, 1701, pp. 807–14

PLUMB, J.H., *England in the Eighteenth Century (1714–1815)*, Harmondsworth (Penguin) 1950

REHN, J.A.G., 'The John Eatton Le Conte collection of paintings of insects, arachnids, and myriapods', *Proceedings of the American Philosophical Society*, 98, 1954, pp. 442–48

REICHER, E., 'Maria Sibylla Merian in Surinam. Commentary to facsimile edition of *Metamorphosis Insectorum Surinamensium* (1705)', London (Pion) 1982

REMINGTON, C., 'Brief biographies, 10: 'Notes on my life'', John Abbot', *The Lepidopterist's News*, **2**, 1944, pp. 28–30

REYNOLDS, E.P., 'John Abbot, pioneer naturalist', *Georgia Review*, **37**, 1983, pp. 816–25

RHOADS, S.N., 'Georgia's rarities further discovered in a second American portfolio of John Abbot's bird plates', *Auk*, **35**, 1918, pp. 271–86

[ROBSON, J.] *Some memoirs of the life and works of George Edwards. Appendix – Catalogue of birds, insects, etc contained in Edwards' Natural History in seven volumes with the Latin names by Linnaeus*, London (J. Robson) 1776

ROGERS, J.V., 'John Abbot, Samuel Wright and a volume of Abbot's watercolours', *The Atlanta Historical Journal*, **22**, 1978, pp. 29–44

ROGERS-PRICE, V., *John Abbot in Georgia: The vision of a naturalist artist (1751–1840)*, exhib. cat., Madison, Madison Morgan Cultural Center, 1983

ROGERS-PRICE,V., 'John Abbot in England and North America: his accomplishments as artist and naturalist', *Turnbull Library Record*, **17**, 1984, pp. 61-80

ROGERS-PRICE, V.A., and GRIFFIN, W.W., 'John Abbot pioneer artist of Georgia', *Antiques*, **124**, 1983, pp. 768–75

ROTHSTEIN, N., 'Joseph Dandridge – naturalist and silk designer', *East London Papers*, **9**, 1966, pp. 102–18

ROUGETEL, H. Le, *The Chelsea Gardener. Philip Miller, 1691–1771*, London (The Natural History Museum) 1990

SAWYER, F.C., 'Notes on some original drawings used by Dr John Latham', *Journal of the Society for the History of Natural History*, **2**, 1949, pp. 173–74

SCHAEFFER, J.C., *Elementa entomologica*, Regensburg 1780

SCUDDER, S.H., 'John Abbot the Aurelian', *Canadian Entomologist*, **20**, 1888, pp. 230–32

SCUDDER, S.H., *Butterflies of the Eastern United States and Canada*, 1, Cambridge, Mass. 1889, pp. 651–54

SHOUMATOFF, A., *Russian Blood: a family chronicle*, New York 1982

SIMPSON, M.B., 'The artist naturalist John Abbot (1751–1840). Contributions to the ornithology of the south-eastern United States', *North Carolina Historical Review*, **61**, 1984, pp. 347–90

SIMPSON, M.B., 'Artistic sources for John Abbot's watercolour drawings of American Birds', *Archives of Natural History*, **20**, 1993, pp. 197–212

SITWELL, S., BUCHANAN, H., and FISHER, J., *Fine bird books, 1700–1900*, London (Collins) 1953

SMEATHMAN, H., *Some account of the Termites which are found in Africa and other hot climates*, London 1781

SMITH, C.H., 'Memoir of Dru Drury', *Naturalists' Library* (ed. W. Jardine), 1, (Introduction to Mammalia), 1845, pp. 1–71

SMITH, J.E., and ABBOT, J., *The Natural History of the rarer Lepidopterous Insects of Georgia*, 2 vols., London 1797

SMITH, J.P., 'Insects and entomologists, their relation to the community at large', *Popular Science Monthly*, **76**, 1910, pp. 469–70

SMITH, R.L., *History of Entomology*, Palo Alto (Annual Reviews Inc.) 1973

SORENSEN, W.C., *Brethren of the Net. American entomology, 1840–1870*, Tuscaloosa and London (University of Alabama Press) 1995

STEARNS, R.P., *Science in the British colonies of America*, Chicago and London (University of Illinois Press) 1970

STONE, W., 'Some unpublished letters of Alexander Wilson and John Abbot', *Auk*, **23**, 1906, pp. 361–68

STRESEMANN, E., 'On a collection of birds from Georgia and Carolina made about 1810 by John Abbot', *Auk*, **70**, 1953, pp. 113–17

STROUD, P.T., *Thomas Say. New World naturalist*, Philadelphia (University of Pennsylvania Press) 1992

SWAINSON, W. 'Taxidermy; Bibliography and Biography', *Cabinet Encyclopedia*, ed. D. Lardner, XII, London 1840, pp. 99–100

TUXEN, S.L., 'The entomologist J.C. Fabricius', *Annual Review of Entomology*, **12**, 1967, pp. 1–14

TUXEN, S.L., 'Entomology systematizes and describes: 1700–1815', in Smith, R.L. (1973)

TUZOV, K.V., *Guide to the Butterflies of Russia and Adjacent Territories*, I, Sofia (Pensoft) 1997, pp. 73–74

WAGSTAFF, E.R., and RUTHERFORD, G., 'Letters from Knowsley Hall', *North Western Naturalist*, 1954, pp. 174–83

WALCKENAER, C.A., *Histoire naturelle des Araneides*, Paris 1805–08

WALTON, W.R., 'Entomological drawings and their draughtsmen. Their relation to the development of economic entomology in the United States', *Proceedings of the Entomological Society of Washington*, **23**, 1921, pp. 70–99

WATKINS, T.H., 'Greening of the Empire. Sir Joseph Banks', *National Geographic Magazine*, **190** (5), 1996, pp. 28–52

WATSON, J.H., 'The history of entomological science', *Annual Report of the Manchester Entomological Society*, **12**, 1914, pp. 24–25

WEISS, H.B., 'Two entomologists of the eighteenth century – Eleazar Albin and Moses Harris', *Science Monthly*, **23**, 1926, pp. 558–60

WEISS, H.B., *The pioneer century of American Entomology*, New Brunswick (privately published) 1936

WHITAKER, K., 'The Culture of Curiosity', in Jardine, N. *et al.* (1996), pp. 75–90

WILKINSON, R.S., 'English entomological methods in the seventeenth and eighteenth centuries', Part 1: '1720', Part 2: 'Wilkes to Dutfield', *Entomologists' Record and Journal of Variation*, **78**, 1966, pp. 143–51, 285–92

WILKINSON, R.S., 'Joseph Dandridge and the first Aurelian Society', *Entomologists' Record and Journal of Variation*, **78**, 1966, pp. 89–94

WILKINSON, R.S., 'Elizabeth Glanville, an early English entomologist', *Entomologists' Gazette*, **17**, 1966, pp. 149–60

WILKINSON, R.S., 'John Abbot's birth date', *Entomologists' Record and Journal of Variation*, **87**, 1975, pp. 125–26

WILKINSON, R.S., 'The death of Benjamin Wilkes and the publication of the English Moths and Butterflies', *Entomologists' Record and Journal of Variation*, **90**, 1978, pp. 6–7

WILKINSON, R.S., 'Smith and Abbot, *The Natural History of the rarer Lepidopterous Insects of Georgia* (1797), and its authorship and history', *Entomologists' Record and Journal of Variation*, **93**, 1981, pp. 213–18; **94**, 1982, pp. 122, 159–60

WILKINSON, R.S., 'In Benjamin Wilkes The British Aurelian *Twelve new designs of English Butterflies and Directions for making a collection*' [facsimile], *Classica Entomologica*, **3**, Faringdon (E.W. Classey Ltd) 1982

WILKINSON, R.S., 'John Abbot's London years' (Parts 1–4), *Entomologists' Record and Journal of Variation*, **96**, 1984, pp. 110–23, 165–76, 222–29, 273–85

WILKES, B., *The English moths and butterflies: Together with the plants and fruits whereon they feed, and are usually found*, London 1747–49

WOODFALL, J.J., 'History of the 13th Earl of Derby's menagerie and aviary at Knowsley Hall, Liverpool (1806–1851)', *Archives of Natural History*, **12**, 1990, pp. 231–52

# Index